D0777173

THINKING ANEW

Gordon Linney

Thinking Anew

Faith in a World of Change and Doubt

the columba press

First published in 2015 by

the columba press

55A Spruce Avenue,
Stillorgan Industrial Park,
Blackrock, Co. Dublin

Cover design by Helene Pertl / The Columba Press
Origination by The Columba Press
Printed by ScandBook AB, Sweden

ISBN 978 1 78218 251 1

In memory of Helen

'To say to someone I love you is to say you will live forever'

Foreword

What person in today's world does not sometimes long for words of comfort, words of inspiration, and words of encouragement? If you are one of these people, then enquire within, as our forefathers would have put it. Open this book and you will find inside all of the above and more, even things that may startle and excite you. Ideas and discourses which will make you think and will encourage you to want to read more. It may even startle the more cynical into rethinking their opinions about religion, about faith, about God.

Gordon Linney is a man of rugged integrity. He is not afraid to tell it like it is: 'The demise of the Celtic Tiger was more a moral failure than an economic failure … a failure to live responsibly as a nation in the light of the values to which we have long paid lip service.' He is not afraid to mention the unmentionable: 'Politics gave way to decency in Dungarvan recently where a memorial was unveiled to the 1100 Waterford men and women … who died in the first World War.' He is not afraid to say what he is thinking: 'When life is hard, believers well understand the desperate cry of the psalmist: 'My God, my God, why, why, why …?' Remembering the sinking of the Titanic, he says: 'This raises the question: where was

God in all this anguish and despair?' He is not afraid to go right to the heart of the matter, reminding us in 'The Way of the World' of the words of Dr Martin Luther King: 'The stumbling block to the Negro's stride for freedom is not the White Citizen's Council or the Ku Klux Klan, but the white moderate who is more devoted to "order" than to justice.' He is not afraid to talk about faith and God in an increasingly secular and scientific world. Gordon Linney is not afraid, and that is what makes so many of these pieces so fascinating and compelling.

And so, from the gentleness of the first piece, 'Music's Measure', the reader is led on a journey of surprise, of comfort, of the unexpected, of the truly disturbing and perhaps most importantly, to moments of challenge. The challenge to think differently about issues of life, faith, God, hope and love for the believer and non-believer alike.

Thinking Anew offers comfort from a writer who captures the zeitgeist of our world and who clearly understands that world – our busy, demanding, anxiety-driven world, where the needs of our inner life, and the life of the spirit, are not always attended to and nourished as they should be. He reminds us in a wonderful piece entitled 'Stephen Street, Dublin 2' of, amongst other things, the origin of the expression to not touch something 'with a forty-foot barge pole', finishing the piece with the following: 'And all this and more, because the Man from Galilee taught us that no one is ever beyond the reach of God's love and care.'

As a counterpoint to this is the challenge laid down in various pieces – 'The Outsider', 'Who Cares', and 'Kristallnacht'. We move from the local to the national to the global: 'The plight of homeless people is clear to anyone walking the streets of our cities. We encounter it in those outstretched hands that silently ask for help – and we don't quite know what to do.' This in turn leads him on to prayer, to the well-known and well-loved Prayer of St Francis, 'for it is by giving that we receive ...'

And then on to 'Kristallnacht' and words from the *New York Times*, 9 November 1938: 'A wave of destruction and looting swept over Germany as National Socialist cohorts took vengeance on Jewish shops, offices and synagogues. Huge, mostly silent crowds looked on and the police confined themselves to regulating traffic.' And Gordon Linney goes on to say of the crowd that gathered, 'and many would probably have claimed to be Christian.'

From here on to the eternal quest, the Science versus Religion debate ('In Search of Truth', 'Science meets Religion', and 'Believing in an Age of Science'). Finally, we can read a measured Christian response to the issue, opening it up to discussion and debate in a reasoned way. Hailing Stephen Hawking – 'This is a man to be honoured and celebrated not only for his courage but also for his intellect: he makes us think.' – Gordon Linney makes us think as he states, 'Some people of faith feel threatened by people like Stephen Hawking, but we should value their searching and questioning.' He addresses the mistaken belief that religious faith and scientific knowledge are incompatible. He takes Richard Dawkins on the chin, invoking the greats, Professor John Polkinghorne, Dr Keith Ward, Dr David Wilkinson, Professor Wilkie Au, Dr Jonathan Sacks, former Chief Rabbi, 'Science is about explanation. Religion is about interpretation.'

Prayer is given its place too, as we are reminded in 'Laborare Est Orare': 'When we pray for someone, something, it does not mean sitting back and doing nothing. Prayers have responsibilities attached.' It moves prayer on from our childlike list of very specific requests to a more mature understanding of what prayer really is, the true nature of prayer. Faith and churchgoing are discussed in 'Last Man Standing': 'There are signs, however, that a religion of convention is giving way to a religion of conviction and commitment. This will happen wherever the Church is faithful to Jesus Christ rather than itself, and wherever people are *living* rather than *discussing* the faith.'

There is nothing facile or simple about these pieces, the thoughts and images planted in our minds will stay with us. They will often lead us back into a second reading of the piece, and prompt a desire to read the books which have inspired the writer's thoughts, not least the Psalms. Gordon Linney has an eye for the great saints and heroes of our world, and is effortlessly able to distil the wisdom of seemingly disparate groups including theologians, philosophers, scientists, thinkers and commentators in a stimulating and accessible way. The clear, unambiguous writing style, in a language that speaks clearly and courageously to the issues of the day, of our day, is very appealing. Even the titles are thought-provoking and intriguing: 'Music's Measure', 'A Frontline Faith', 'Prayer Understood', 'Things That Last', 'Beyond the Pain'.

Let me end with a fervent prayer: Thank you God, for the sheer pleasure of books such as this, books which we can treasure, books which we can hold in our hands, keep on the bedside table, share with our families and give to our friends as gifts! Amen.

Rev. Olive Donohoe

Acknowledgements

I wish to acknowledge the help and support of the many people who made this book possible.

First of all *The Irish Times* for allowing me the privilege of writing these columns over the years. My thanks to the editor Kevin O'Sullivan and his personal assistant Lynda O'Keeffe for their support; special thanks also to Patsy McGarry and former Letters Page Editor Liam McAuley for their guidance in my early days.

I have been greatly helped by my publishers Columba Press. I am extremely grateful for the advice and support given by the team there. They were always professional, helpful and perhaps most important, a pleasure to work with.

I am also grateful to Ross Hinds for his helpful advice and encouragement.

A book like this is shaped in some measure by the experiences of the people where one has worked over the years. I am therefore indebted to the people of Agherton Parish, Portstewart and Down Cathedral, Downpatrick where I served in the troubled seventies; also to the people of St Catherine's and St James' parishes in Dublin's Liberties, a very special place and Glenageary Parish, a community with so much to give.

Finally to place on record my deep debt to my late wife Helen and our children Susan, Heather and David, all of whom in different ways have given me a lifetime of support and encouragement.

Contents

Introduction

This book contains a selection of pieces written by me for *The Irish Times* Saturday column *Thinking Anew*.

Each one was written with the ordinary man or woman in the street in mind – churchgoer and non-churchgoer alike. They were never intended to tell anyone what to think but rather to encourage people to think for themselves. The churches struggle to get their message across often because they don't speak in language that people understand or the message as presented does not connect with everyday life. Religion makes no sense at all if it does not help us to understand and deal with what's going on in our lives. The theologian Karl Barth said that clergy should preach with the Bible in one hand and the newspaper in the other.

I have drawn on the insights and experiences not only of writers and thinkers with a Christian background but some from other faith traditions, so in the best and fullest sense of the word I can say this is a truly ecumenical work. In no way could it be described as denominational.

There is, however, something personal about some of the pieces. I retired from active ministry in 2004 to care for my wife, Helen, who had suffered from Parkinson's disease for many years. In time she became totally dependent on me and some of my writing reflects that situation; a person of faith, trying to make sense of a religion of hope in what seemed at times like a hopeless situation. I have not been disappointed.

Gordon Linney

Music's Measure

Celebrating the life of Wolfgang Amadeus Mozart, in particular his contribution to liturgical music, on the 250th anniversary of his birth.

Published 4 February 2006

Music lovers worldwide have been celebrating the 250th anniversary of the birth of Wolfgang Amadeus ('beloved of God') Mozart in Salzburg on 27 January 1756. Considered by many to be the greatest of all the composers, he has left a superb treasury of music which has inspired and uplifted generations.

It was appropriate that last Sunday morning Dublin's Pro-Cathedral marked the anniversary with a performance of the *Spatzen Mass*, K220, the first in a series of ten Mozart masses to be performed this year. Church recognition is important for several reasons. First of all Mozart served the Church. An early employer of his was the Archbishop at Salzburg, whose views on the role of the church musician did not always coincide with those of the talented young man (a not unknown phenomenon in church affairs). The Archbishop tried to control and at times suppress Mozart, who rebelled and was ejected from his post, some say physically. Despite these difficulties – and his later spiritual wanderings – Mozart has left us a rich store of religious and liturgical music.

Secondly, music written for the Mass is best heard in a church setting. Concert hall performances are fine but they lack the structure of the liturgy, the spoken word that explains, that creates space and mood and connects the listener in a personal way to what is being performed. To the man or woman of faith, the Kyrie, for example, is more than a pleasant-sounding piece of music. It is a cry for mercy by someone who is conscious of his or her personal unworthiness.

Mozart was a genuinely religious man. Writing to his father, he comforted him by saying, 'God is ever before my eyes. I realise his omnipotence and I fear his anger; but I also recognise his love, his compassion and his tenderness towards his creatures.' Commenting on the conduct of his contemporaries he observed: 'I cannot possibly live like the majority of our young men. In the first place I have too much religion; in the second too much love for my fellow man and too great a sense of honour.' He could also be critical of the excesses of the ruling elite, as this comment makes clear: 'The heart shows the true nobleman, and although I am not a count, I am more honourable perhaps than many a count …' It has been suggested that this criticism finds expression in the plot and the characters in the *Marriage of Figaro*.

As we celebrate the genius of the man, it is worth reflecting on its inspiration and its source. To some, it will seem possible to one day be able to explain genius, and possibly even replicate it when it is finally known how the human brain works. But others will find the explanation elsewhere, as Karl Barth, the twentieth-century Swiss theologian and passionate admirer of Mozart, did. It is said that Barth began each day listening to Mozart's music for at least half an hour. Here he suggests its significance and its status: 'The golden sounds and melodies of Mozart's music have from early times spoken to me not as gospel but as parables of the realms of God's free grace as revealed in the gospel – and they do so again with great spontaneity and directness.'

This encourages us to believe that in celebrating the life and work of Wolfgang Amadeus Mozart we are celebrating nothing less than the free gift of a loving and generous God.

> *Next to theology I give to music the highest place and honour. Music is the art of the prophets, the only art that can calm the agitations of the soul; it is one of the most magnificent and delightful presents God has given us.*
>
> *(Martin Luther)*

To Bethlehem

*We tend to overlook the challenges that are so clearly represented in the
Christmas story.*

Christmas Eve 2005

After the past few busy weeks, Christmas Eve brings relief as
preparations are completed and we begin to think of celebration.
Celebration comes easily to those for whom Christmas is a time to
be enjoyed with family and friends. For others in different
circumstances it can mean sadness and loneliness, a time mainly for
memories. However, Christmas, properly understood, has meaning
for everyone if we recall what it is we really celebrate. We do not
turn in heart and mind to Bethlehem each year to find an excuse for
a party or even to be reminded that we should be generous and
caring. Instead, we go there to learn about the living God, who
promises to be with us in all circumstances of life.

It was once said of a distinguished cleric that for six days of the
week in his parish he was invisible, and on the seventh day in the

pulpit he was incomprehensible. The one was the consequence of the other: without the human touch, religion becomes a cold philosophy. Theology only comes alive when it connects with flesh and blood, as St John tells us in the incarnation, 'the Word became flesh and dwelt among us'. Christians believe that the amazing truth at the heart of Christmas is that God, in order to be comprehensible, became visible, and shared our human life fully from the cradle to the grave and beyond.

The story of Bethlehem has its shining lights, but it has its dark side too. One of the details that stands out is that there was no room for them in the inn. Imagine the innkeeper with a full house and not an inch to spare anywhere. There is nothing to suggest that he was mean or uncaring. He was probably a decent, hard-working man, but he is remembered two thousand years on as the man who said 'no'. And the irony is that while at one level he excluded Mary and Joseph, at the much deeper level he excluded himself from having a part in events that were to change the world. It is too easy to say 'no' to things we have little time for, have not thought through or do not value sufficiently. Christmas is a time to think afresh, to reflect on the truths embedded in the Bethlehem story and all that flows from it. We may ask questions about the historicity of certain details as they have come down to us, but no one can deny that Jesus was born and lived and died, and that his life has profoundly affected the course of human history.

Earlier this month, admirers of the late John Lennon marked the 25th anniversary of his tragic death in New York. When the Beatles were at the height of their fame it was claimed that they were more popular than Jesus Christ. But tonight and tomorrow countless millions around the world will gather to celebrate the birth of Jesus Christ, as people have done for centuries.

The stable birth is a symbol of an important aspect of the Christmas story that is easily overlooked. The young couple, despite their desperate plight, were pushed to one side and left to fend for themselves and to find what shelter they could. Unlike the cosy stable scenes we see on Christmas cards, where they ended up was grim. And they were there not only because the inn was full but because there was no room in people's hearts for the compassion that would have recognised their plight. That aspect of the Christmas story challenges us to be responsive to the needs of vulnerable people around us. And just as importantly for those who feel that Christmas is not for them, it is worth remembering that this festival is a celebration of the fact that God's coming among us brought him closest to those who were told there was no room for them. In God's world there is room for everyone.

The Word of God, Jesus Christ, on account of his great love for humankind, became what we are in order to make us what He is himself.

(St Irenaeus)

Having Nothing, Yet Possessing All Things

Until you make peace with who you are, you'll never be content with what you have.

Published 4 March 2006

Lent is about something more radical and important than giving up some modest pleasure for a few weeks and then getting back to what is considered normal. It is an invitation to reflect deeply about self, and the values and priorities that control our lives. It is a discipline based on the temptations of Jesus in the wilderness.

There is a contemporary ring to what is on offer in that wilderness event: power, wealth, celebrity status. These are very real and present attractions to many in modern, prosperous Ireland; the issue, however, is not about having them, but how we use them. There is a vast difference between *possessing* something and *being possessed by* it.

Jesus alerts us to this danger. In St Luke's Gospel we are told he commends the poor, saying: 'Blessed are those of you who are poor.'

To us such a remark may seem surprising; to the people of that time it was daft. For them, prosperity was a sign of God's approval, whereas poverty was a disgrace, a sign of God's disfavour. But Jesus challenged this. He pronounced a blessing on the hungry, the sad and the persecuted, and commiserated with the well-off, the happy and the popular. Thus, in those few words he demolished the general beliefs of the average man or woman, who, if asked, would probably say that what they wanted most from life was a good job, a good home and a reasonable lifestyle.

A positive view of poverty for poverty's sake is hard to make sense of, especially for anyone who has known the reality of it in Ireland or overseas. For example, watching hundreds of AIDS orphans, some as young as four, gather at a church school playground in Uganda to collect a thin foam mattress roll and little else, then head off into the distance in little family groups hoping that someone, somewhere would give them food and shelter; that kind of desperate poverty is deeply troubling to the observer and has nothing to commend it.

But Jean Vanier, a man who has dedicated his life to caring for the disabled and the disadvantaged, makes this significant comment: 'This option for the poor is not to say Jesus loves some people more than others, but rather that he rejoices with those who open their hearts to him … they welcome him; they have time to listen to him and to rejoice in him. The rich often seem too busy: they think they have everything they need; they feel self-sufficient … they create a false world made up of pretence and appearance. They have no time to waste on Jesus. They have better things to do; making and defending wealth, exercising power!'

That kind of obsession has a strong element of self-destruction built into it. We can see this, for example, in the attitude of various powerful interests, national and international, in the reckless exploitation of the environment. Closed and selfish minds ignore serious warnings about damage being done to the planet, and the consequences this will have for our children and their children. We nod disapprovingly but not enough to accept the necessary political action, or the inevitable changes to the way we live. That same destructive element can touch us even more intimately and personally when we allow personal ambition and career interests to take precedence over relationships and family life. It is so easy to end up having everything and having nothing.

Jesus was not opposed to the notion of wealth and the enjoyment of it, in fact, it is clear from the gospel that he had rich friends and supporters and enjoyed their company. However, he does warn about the dangers of neglecting our spiritual needs, and of allowing selfishness to take control of our lives to the exclusion of other important and more valuable treasures. The Christian concept of self-denial, which is emphasised in Lent, is not a call to morbid living but a process of self-discovery in which we come to know our real selves and the things that contribute to our well-being. Lent is only a starter course; self-denial is a lifelong journey.

The true value of a human being is determined primarily by the measure and the sense in which he has attained liberation from the self.

(Albert Einstein)

A Frontline Faith

The fiftieth anniversary of the end of World War II in Europe.

Published 15 May 2005 (Pentecost)

In recent weeks, many have been thinking back to the Second World War with mixed emotions. Those who lived through it will be conscious of the terrible cost in human terms, while recalling at the same time the joy and the hope that marked its ending.

Looking back, thinking people of all ages must surely be aware that the moral ascent of man to higher and nobler things is never assured, but has to be worked for – Belsen and Auschwitz have proved that beyond a doubt.

A correspondent of the time courageously pointed out that the atrocities of WWII were not just a failing of the German people but a failing of humanity. However, it was not a total failure, even within Germany. While we focus on the generalities – the great battles and political developments, the winners and losers – there are other important matters to keep in mind. We know, for example, of many

26

courageous people in Germany and elsewhere who stood out against the monstrous evils of the day, often at great cost to themselves and their families. Many of them are unknown and unsung, and were motivated by strong religious and moral conviction.

Dietrich Bonhoeffer, a Lutheran Pastor, was one of the leading young theologians of his day and had an international reputation. By 1936, however, he had been banned from teaching by the Nazis and a year later the seminary of which he was head was closed. Bonhoeffer fell out of favour by opposing the German-Christians (Deutsche Christen), a powerful evangelical group who were advocating an interpretation of Christianity that could accommodate Nazism. He joined what was known as the Confessing Church, which laid the foundation for resistance to attempts to make the Evangelical Churches instruments of Nazi policy. In 1942 he tried to mediate between those Germans opposed to Hitler and the British Government but he was arrested and sent to Buchenwald.

Bonhoeffer was adamant that no political system could supersede in any way the authority and meaning of Jesus Christ. Writing about the cross he commented, 'God's victory ... means reducing the world and its clamour to silence; it means the crossing out of all ideas and plans, it means the cross. The cross of Jesus Christ means the bitter scorn of all human heights, the bitter suffering of God in all human depths, the rule of God over the whole world.' In a message to an English friend, he also said, 'I believe in the principle of our universal Christian brotherhood which rises above all national interests, and that our victory is certain.'

Bonhoeffer was sentenced to death and was hanged on Good Friday 1945. He was thirty-nine years old. Not long before his execution, some of his fellow prisoners, who were greatly encouraged by his firm preaching of the Easter Hope, asked him to conduct a service for them. When he was finished he was taken away. Later a prison doctor observed him kneeling in prayer. 'The devotion and evident conviction of being heard that I saw in this intensely captivating man,' the doctor recorded, 'moved me to the depths.'

Tomorrow is the Feast of Pentecost, that day when Christians give thanks for the gift of the Holy Spirit. We can too easily diminish this extraordinary presence by relegating its activity to things that in a narrow way are perceived to be religious. The Spirit is not owned or controlled by the Church or anyone else. The Spirit is available in all places, at all times, to all people of goodwill, who seek to make known to the world 'the wonderful works of God'. It is good to remember in these days of special, and sometimes painful, memories that even in the darkest days of a world at war the Spirit of peace was present. It was active in and through the life of Dietrich Bonhoeffer, and others like him.

Where God Is

The God who is above all and in all: a lesson learned while visiting Kisiizi Hospital Uganda.

Published 28 May 2006 (Ascension)

On 12 April 1961, a Russian major, Yuri Gagarin, became the first human being to travel in space. At the time it was widely publicised that he had reported back from space that he did not see 'any god up here'. This is disputed, however, and people close to Gagarin insist that he was a committed Christian and would not say such a thing. They attribute the remark, with some supporting evidence, to Nikita Khrushchev, the Russian leader of the time. Speaking at a party meeting to promote anti-religious propaganda, Khrushchev argued that when Gagarin was in space he did not see God there. This episode reminds us of a problem we sometimes have with religious language and outdated imagery. The issue between Khrushchev and Gagarin was a case of altitude versus attitude.

Khrushchev was anti-belief and poked fun at a childish picture of God seated above the clouds.

The distinction between altitude and attitude is helpful when we think about the Feast of the Ascension celebrated on Thursday. Where do we seek or find God? Where is Jesus present and active? In the Book of Acts the 'men of Galilee' are admonished and asked why they stand looking up into heaven.

The Ascension is a dividing line between two kinds of presence, rather than between presence and absence. It marks the transition from a localised physical presence to a universal presence. The former relates to his presence when he walked the roads of Palestine and engaged directly with the people he met. That ministry was inevitably limited in terms of time and space, linked to the physical location of Jesus at any given time. Indeed, when Lazarus died his sisters were upset that Jesus was not there when they needed him and the gospel records show that the disciples had a real fear of losing that presence.

After the Ascension, the Church had to learn that this same ministry of Jesus continued at a universal level through the Church, where he is present in a sacramental way. And here is the difficult bit: the presence is not restricted to a liturgical event. It has to be seen for real in the lives of the faithful and in that way made known to the wider world. The motivation for this is God's love for the world and his desire to rescue and heal a confused and broken humanity. Sadly, too often we Christians become part of the problem rather than the solution. However, despite our failings the spirit of Jesus is never quenched and his compassion and goodness are expressed through the lives and work of faithful people every day.

I had the privilege of visiting a hospital in a remote part of southwest Uganda near the Congo border. Kisiizi Hospital is a Christian foundation dating from the 1950s, where extraordinary work is done for sick people in an area of great need. The majority of the staff are

Ugandan, but they are assisted by some dedicated European doctors, nurses and other professionals. These people, at great cost in personal and financial terms, help make the healing Christ present and real to the people of this area. Everyone who works in Kisiizi Hospital does so because they believe that God has called them to this work in this place. There are thousands of similar projects across the globe, all done in the name and power of Jesus Christ.

Writing about the disciples and Ascension the Rev. John Stott says: 'There was something fundamentally anomalous about their gazing up into the sky when they had been commissioned to go to the ends of the earth. It was the earth, not the sky, that was to be their preoccupation. Their calling was to be witnesses, not stargazers.' It is no different for us today.

On a side note: whatever Major Gagarin may or may not have said about God it is interesting that on Christmas Eve 1968 the crew of the American *Apollo 8* spacecraft, the first humans to travel beyond the influence of Earth's gravity and view the moon close-up, were so struck by what they saw that as the people of the world watched live images of the lunar surface, each of the three crewmen read from the Book of Genesis. In that case, attitude and altitude seem to have been in agreement.

Learning From The Past

The terrible cost of war: remembering with a purpose.

Published 11 November 2006 (Remembrance Day)

The name Ronald Mallett will probably mean little or nothing to people today. He was, however, world famous in his day as a boy soprano for a recording of Mendelssohn's 'I Waited for the Lord', which he made in 1927 with the even-more-famous Ernest Lough. Both were choristers at London's Temple Church, but beyond that their futures differed greatly. Lough continued his singing career as an adult at the Temple Church, where in time he was joined by his son. Ronald Mallett had a very different experience: he died tragically young in a Japanese prisoner of war camp in 1945, his wonderful talent and life's potential extinguished. That is what war does in human terms. Again and again, whether in Ireland or continental Europe, Vietnam or Iraq, it destroys too much that is innocent and beautiful.

This weekend, in many places women and men will pause to remember the countless millions who have suffered and died as a result of war. To those closely involved, memories will inevitably be personal and to some extent selective. But for those who remember in a less personal way it is important to remember that the grim consequences of human conflict recognise no boundaries – religious, political or ideological. National or religious jingoism, prompted by the notion that 'God is on our side' is both dangerous and inhuman, in that it allows us to think that some lives matter less than others.

The importance of rising above such sentiments was illustrated in July 1982, when the then Archbishop of Canterbury, Dr Robert Runcie led a special service in St Paul's Cathedral in London to mark the end of the Falklands War. It is said he displeased many, including some senior members of the political establishment, when he acknowledged Argentinian losses. He said, 'In our prayers we shall quite rightly remember those who are bereaved in our own country, and the relations of the young Argentinian soldiers who were killed. Common sorrow could do something to reunite those who were engaged in this struggle.' He went on to say, 'War has always been detestable. It is impossible to be a Christian and not to long for peace.' The Archbishop knew what he was talking about, having seen active service in World War II, and witnessed for himself the notorious camp at Belsen.

In the gospels, we are given insights into the attitude of Jesus towards physical force. We are told that he instructed Peter to put his sword away when he tried to defend Jesus at the time of his arrest. Previously he had wept over Jerusalem, and said that the city and its citizens faced destruction because they neglected the things that belonged to their peace.

A special prayer provided for tomorrow's liturgy speaks of the families of nations divided and torn apart by the ravages of sin, and asks that they may be subject to God's just and gentle rule. However, that rule is frustrated where we ignore the things that belong to our peace and tolerate such things as economic injustice, the denial of human rights or the promotion of racial and religious hatreds.

A creative remembrance can be an opportunity not only to deal with personal loss, which is of course important, but also to take a wider view to acknowledge the awfulness of war and what it does to people no matter who they are. And perhaps most importantly in this troubled world, where our best efforts seem to fail so often, the words recorded almost eighty years ago by Ronald Mallett, that London choirboy, remind us that we are not alone: 'I waited for the Lord, he inclined unto me. O blest are they that hope and trust in him' (Psalm 40).

War should belong to the tragic past, to history. It should find no place on humanity's agenda for the future.

(Pope John Paul II)

If I Were A Rich Man

Money is not the root of all evil; loving it can be.

Published 14 October 2006

In the musical *Fiddler on the Roof*, Tevye is a Jewish peasant milkman in pre-revolutionary Russia whose circumstances are rather uncertain. He is the character who sings 'If I Were a Rich Man' as he contemplates all the good things that could come his way if only God would allow him to have even a small fortune. He would not have to work hard, he could build a big house and his wife could put on airs and strut around like a peacock. Many have dreamed the same dream.

The subject of wealth is dealt with in the Gospel of Mark (10:17–22). A young man, full of good intentions, asks Jesus what he must do to inherit eternal life. Jesus lists a number of the commandments and the inquirer assures him that he has observed them all.

Then Jesus tells him to sell what he owns and give the money to the poor. We are told the young man went away sorrowful, for he had many possessions.

Jesus goes on to say that it is easier for a camel to go through the eye of a needle than for a rich man to enter the kingdom of God. This has often been taken as a reference to a narrow entrance gate to the city of Jerusalem through which a camel bearing side loads could not pass. However, this is disputed, and many hold that there is no evidence that such a gate ever existed. The illustration taken literally is much more powerful, given that it is intended to show that the exercise is impossible.

But what is impossible? Are we, for example, to take it that Jesus is saying that it is impossible for any rich person to enter the kingdom of God simply because he or she is rich; that wealth itself is automatically an obstacle to spiritual growth?

It is important to remember that his audience was brought up on the Old Testament, in which wealth was often seen as a sign of God's approval. The disciples are shocked because they think that if a rich man cannot be saved then what chance have they. It is a teaching not unheard of even today, yet Jesus challenges this, and the Christian view is that all are equal before God whatever their status or wealth. But the question remains: what is impossible?

One of the most misquoted verses in the Bible deals with money. It is often said that money is the root of all evil. George Bernard Shaw thought the contrary: 'The lack of money is the root of all evil.' The actual text tells us that it is the love of money that is the root of all evil. That is an important distinction, because money itself is morally neutral. It is neither good nor evil, and only becomes a problem when it takes control of us and possesses us. That is the issue in that encounter between Jesus and a well-intentioned young man who wanted to do better, but whose attachment to wealth stood in the way. This is not just about money; it is a warning against any desire or ambition that could take control of our lives – say, for example, the desire for power or influence or status. These are real issues in the Ireland of today.

Christianity is not opposed to the possession of wealth as such but it does encourage its responsible and creative use. Take for example, Alfred Nobel, the Swedish chemist who invented dynamite. As a hugely successful industrialist Nobel acquired great wealth, but some time before his death a newspaper inadvertently published his obituary in which he was described as a 'merchant of death' because of his association with dynamite. It is said he was much troubled by this and altered his will to provide a considerable fortune to set up the Nobel Foundation. To this day, the organisation awards prizes to men and women who have made outstanding contributions to society in the fields of physics, chemistry, literature, medicine and, significantly for him, peace. Perhaps he was familiar with the words of Socrates: 'If a rich man is proud of his wealth, he should not be praised until it is known how he employs it.'

Listen Here

Before we can be a serving church we must learn to be a listening church.

Published 28 October 2006

There is a tendency for some religious people to picture a God who is hugely interested in the religious aspects of life, but less interested in its everyday facets. He is a Sunday God, one who is associated with the church building and all that goes on there but has little to do with the factory or the office block. As the Anglican priest F. D. Maurice, who was deeply involved with the Christian Socialist movement, complained over a hundred years ago: 'We have been dosing our people with religion, when what they want is not that, but the living God.'

In our fast-moving, changing society it is not always easy to engage. Within the Church, too much time and energy are absorbed in sustaining outdated and sometimes redundant structures that no longer work. This is compounded by a temptation to see religion as a means of escape from a world that seems at times less and less attractive. This of course can be quite selfish, and unfortunately there are some approaches to spirituality that tend to reinforce the idea. However, intimacy with God, which is what spirituality is about, directs us towards where people are, to reflect his love and gentleness in a harsh unforgiving world. A hymn by Timothy Rees makes the point: 'God is love … and when human hearts are breaking, under sorrow's iron rod, then they find that self-same aching deep within the heart of God.' Christians believe that God feels and understands human suffering and uses faithful people to ease it.

Those who insist that the Church should confine itself to something called 'religion' have little understanding of the Christian sense of the God who is everywhere and in and through everything. Harvey Cox, the American theologian, insists that God is just as present in the secular as in the religious realms of life. He questions the Church's role as a protective religious institution, isolated from the world. Instead, he suggests that it should be in the forefront of change in society, discovering the new ways that faith can impact on the world of today.

In the Gospel of St Mark (10:46–52), the encounter between Jesus and a blind man called Bartimeus has something useful to say to the Church about how to engage with the world. Jesus is leaving Jericho and is followed by a large crowd. When Bartimeus is told Jesus is passing he calls out for help, but is told by the crowd to be quiet. He persists until Jesus hears him and asks a simple but beautiful question: What do you want me to do for you? The man asks for his sight and he receives it.

Can the church of today live with a question like that: what do you want me to do for you? It is so much easier to tell people what they must do for the Church, and how they must conform to convention and to social and moral standards. It is easy to be a demanding church; so much more difficult and costly to be a listening, under-standing and serving church.

Bartimeus had a limited understanding of Jesus, but this did not disqualify him from making an approach. He was received and welcomed. There are lots of people who do not understand or cannot sign up fully to traditional teaching about Jesus, and yet who see in him someone of great significance for them.

In 'The One' Patrick Kavanagh reminds us of the living God who is always out there, with or without us, available to people in the most unlikely of places: 'God is down in the swamps and marshes … A humble scene in a backward place … breathing His love by a cut-away bog.'

⌾

A Church Divided

Have we lost our way ecumenically? The Octave of Prayer for Christian Unity.

Published 20 January 2007

Has the modern ecumenical movement lost its way? No one can deny that at grass-roots level there is new warmth and friendship, and that is great gain. But at a leadership level, nationally and internationally, it is not so easy to discern progress. There is resistance to change and if the Church is to address the needs of the modern world we need to pay more attention to the leading of the Spirit. The decline in religious influence has more to do with the rejection of a discredited church than a discredited gospel.

For many, the ecumenical movement is an internal process intended to solve doctrinal disagreements and address organisational issues to do with authority and ministry. These are important but ecumenism is not just about churches agreeing with each other. Far more important is the Church's mission which is to show a bitterly divided world that Christians have the secret of living in peace with difference and diversity. Jesus said that his authentic followers would be identified, not by doctrinal consistency or loyalty to one church structure or another, but by the fact that they loved one another: 'All will know that you are my disciples if you love one another' (St John 13:35). Church history is littered with examples of failures to do so.

In an upper room in Belfast some years ago a church group of which I was a member met three leaders of loyalism to talk about peace. Among them was the late David Ervine. I asked him what the churches could do to help. His response was direct and challenging: 'A plague on all your houses.' Clearly, these were words of frustration from a man now committed to reconciliation, but who felt that over the years the churches had divided people, especially poor people, and kept them apart for their own purposes. There is reluctance within the churches in Ireland to acknowledge this failure and its consequences.

The ecumenical movement faces a simple question: to what extent do any of our twenty-first century churches measure up to what Jesus Christ intended? When we compare the conduct and values of Jesus with the conduct and values of the institutional church today, we can see that something has seriously gone astray. Somehow the genius and flair of Christianity does not always seem to be at home in our ecclesiastical structures. It is clear from the gospels that Jesus meant to simplify religion and not to complicate it, to assist rather than confuse people and to set them free. He had no time for theological flab. But too many who set out to extend his work decided that his message needed intellectualising if it was to be preserved and that his offer of freedom had to be controlled. So the adventurous religion called Christianity that was supposed to turn the world upside down was tamed and gradually brought under control; the church of the Spirit was made subservient to the church of authority, where dogma and conformity reigned. We need within the Church to rediscover guiding principles and controlling values. Would, for example, the Jesus of the gospels, who spurned material wealth and worldly power, be comfortable and fulfilled within any of our churches? Would he be considered orthodox given some of our doctrinal positions? Would he exclude from his company those that we have difficulty accepting?

In Luke's Gospel (4:16–21), we hear Jesus reading from the scriptures in the synagogue in his home town of Nazareth: 'The Spirit of the Lord is upon me, for he has anointed me to bring good news to the poor ... to proclaim release to the captives ... to let the oppressed go free.' His was a message for humanity that would disturb many (very often religious) people who saw him as a threat to their position and power, and possibly still do.

The church of the Spirit encourages us to look to Jesus: the church of authority tempts us to look no further than itself. Many do not look any further than the Church and are fulfilled, some perhaps unaware that the Church at times demands less than the Jesus of the gospel, who commands us to love totally and unconditionally.

That is not to say that our different understandings and faith experiences are not important or that our traditions and ways of doing things don't have a place; however, where they are allowed to dominate, creative ecumenism cannot proceed.

What matters in the Church is not religion but the form of Christ and its taking form amidst a band of men.
                                                        (Dietrich Bonhoeffer)

Silent Witness

In June 2007 London was brought to a standstill when two car bombs were discovered.

Published 7 July 2007

As news broke of the bomb plots in London, television reports showed images of a deserted city centre, empty of people and traffic. The famous and usually hectic Piccadilly Circus was, in Words-worth's words, 'silent, bare' – but for all the wrong reasons. The poet had in mind the 'beauty of the morning' – whereas this was an imposed silence, created by a cruel desire to kill and maim as many innocent people as possible, irrespective of age, creed or nationality. Evil, for a while, was centre stage. It was an evil that was justified for some due to the corruption of religion, in this case Islam. It is a disease common to all religions, a point well illustrated from the pages of history, not least in Ireland.

In troubling times long ago the psalmist asked 'who can show us any good?' It's a question that never goes away; yet it is not without an answer, for even there in that menacing silence in Piccadilly Circus there was a witness to something better.

Piccadilly is the site of a statue popularly but mistakenly known as *Eros*. Its correct title is *The Angel of Christian Charity*. It is part of the Shaftesbury Memorial, which was erected in 1893 to commemorate the philanthropic works of Anthony Cooper, seventh Earl of Shaftesbury. A politician of influence and a committed Christian, Cooper had a passion for human rights and social justice and campaigned throughout the nineteenth century for social and economic reform. Cooper championed factory legislation and succeeded in ending the employment underground of women and children under thirteen years of age. A friend of Florence Nightingale, he supported health reform, especially for the mentally ill. He was also a founder of the Ragged Schools Union which in a short space of time provided shelter and education to some three hundred thousand poor children in London. Many of the reforms he pioneered still impact on the way we live today. That scene in Piccadilly Circus reminds us that while one person motivated by hatred is capable of much harm, another inspired by the God of love can do great good.

An ecumenical group of lay people and clergy working in South America met to consider the overwhelming challenges they were facing and how these impacted on their faith and spirituality. Most were disillusioned, 'confronted with so much pain, so much abuse, so many empty words, so much corruption and the cruelty of the armed man living off threats, assaults and arrogance'. They recalled a time past when in churches and schools people learned how to be open to each other; how to share; how to live together; how to love; how to assume and ease the pain of others. Looking at the world around them, it was clear that things had changed: 'There are other gospels now. Consume. Be satisfied. They proclaim the sanctity of greed, the 'right' of the powerful to crush others, selling spiritual nostrums to calm inner clamour, dispensing sacramental drugs to assuage fear.'

In one sense there is nothing new in this gloomy assessment – some of it will sound all too familiar – but it represents a real challenge to people of goodwill not to lose heart. St Luke's Gospel (10:3 ff) tells us that Jesus had no illusions about the difficulties his followers would face: 'I am sending you out as lambs in the midst of wolves.' They would be welcomed by some and rejected by others. Nowhere did he ever say his way would be easy; it would be easier perhaps to give up. Yet experience teaches that faithful individuals can and do make a difference by reflecting even a little light in a world which too often is shrouded in darkness.

The crowds are back in Piccadilly Circus. *The Angel of Christian Charity* is there too reminding us of a man whose Christian faith inspired him to do great things for God and for humanity. As Cooper explained to a friend: 'My religious views are not very popular but they are the views that have sustained and comforted me all through my life. I think a man's religion, if it is worth anything, should enter into every sphere of life, and rule his conduct in every relation.'

Forgiving and Forgiven

By any standard the late Gordon Wilson was a remarkable man. His instant willingness to forgive those who murdered his daughter in the Enniskillen Remembrance Day bombing was applauded worldwide but the cost to him personally was huge.

Published 3 March 2007

Twenty years ago, Gordon Wilson lay in the rubble of the Enniskillen bomb, tightly holding the hand of his daughter Marie as she died. Later that evening he gave an emotional account of her last words; then, to the astonishment of the world, he went on to forgive his daughter's killers, and to plead that there would be no revenge for her death. 'I bear no ill will. I bear no grudge. Dirty sort of talk is not going to bring her back to life. I will pray for these men tonight and every night.' He was a modest, humble man, often describing himself as 'only a wee draper from Enniskillen' but to the world looking on he was someone and something much more significant. What they saw was not only a man with a deep Christian faith but one with the grace to forgive those who had so cruelly hurt him and his family. In that moment he underlined the unique characteristic of forgiveness that is a willingness on the part of the aggrieved person, the victim, to accept personally the cost of the wrong or the harm done.

That is what makes it so difficult for so many to forgive; it seems unreasonable that those who have been maltreated by others should be expected to go that far. Instead they demand sympathy and justice, and who is to blame them. There were other victims of the Enniskillen bomb and similar atrocities, decent people, who understandably could not respond like Gordon Wilson.

The South African author Laurens van der Post spent several years as a war prisoner of the Japanese. Writing of his experiences of that harsh regime he said: 'It was amazing how often and how many of my men would confess to me after some ... excess worse than usual, that for the first time in their lives they had realised ... the dynamic power of the first of the crucifixion utterances: "Forgive them for they know not what they do."' He saw forgiveness as a consequence of understanding rather than an expression of religious sentimentality. It was a liberating force within. He put forgiveness firmly in place as the very basis of a meaningful life. It is not optional; it is an essential feature of personal development and growth. To harbour resentment and bitterness is to die a little. To forgive, however difficult, is to grow; it frees up for better things the energy required to nurse grudges and bitterness.

In Christian teaching we are reminded that we all need forgiveness, for, as St Paul tells us, 'all have sinned and fall short of the glory of God' (Romans 3:23). Many will know what the apostle has in mind when he talks about doing the thing he hates and neglecting what is good. We are too easily inclined to think that our personal failings are not all that serious, much like the man in St Luke's Gospel (18:11) who thanked God he wasn't as bad as the people around him. In our own minds, we imagine a league of sinners with ourselves not requiring forgiveness as others do. However, every time we say the Lord's Prayer, we are reminded that forgiveness of our sins is governed by our ability and willingness to forgive those who have wronged us. Our deficiency in this regard – as a nation and as individuals – was a significant factor in the events that caused Gordon Wilson and countless others so much grief and loss.

Reinhold Niebuhr, the American theologian believed that forgiveness was the ultimate expression of love. His words on the subject are worth taking to heart: 'Nothing worth doing is completed in our lifetime; therefore we are saved by hope. Nothing true or beautiful or good makes complete sense in any immediate context of history; therefore we are saved by faith. Nothing we do, however virtuous, can be accomplished alone; therefore we are saved by love. No virtuous act is quite as virtuous from the standpoint of our friend or foe as from our own; therefore we are saved by the final form of love, which is forgiveness.'

Let My People Go

John Newton wrote the words of 'Amazing Grace' – one of the world's best known and best loved hymns – as a result of his remarkable escape from death on a storm-ravaged ship off the Donegal coast which found shelter in Lough Swilly. He was convinced that God had spared him for a purpose.

Published 17 March 2007

'Amazing Grace' has an interesting background. Prior to his religious conversion, its author, John Newton, had been a sea captain engaged in the transportation of African slaves. The hymn is an acknowledgement of both his cruel past and the transformation that religion had meant for him. The journey from slave ship to pulpit (he was ordained in 1764) was for him the result of God's amazing grace. *Companion to the Church Hymnal* (Darling and Davison) makes the point that it was ironic that this hymn, written by a former eighteenth-century slave trader, should become one of the songs of the American civil rights movement two centuries later.

His story and his hymn suggest that God never gives up on anybody; that there is always the hope and the possibility of change and restoration. The gospel story about the return of the Prodigal Son (St Luke 15:11–32) makes the same point. To some there is an aspect of this story that is unfair: that the son who stayed at home and helped over the years was hard done by compared to his brother, who had taken off and indulged himself at his father's expense. It is difficult not to have some empathy with this view because similar situations occur in everyday life; those who stay at home to provide support often feel taken for granted, while those who are absent are applauded and even rewarded.

The story of the Prodigal, however, is not about someone who was absent; it is about someone who was missing and, more importantly, who was missed. There is a difference. When we see reports of missing persons and listen to distraught family members appeal for information, we can only imagine what they are going through, especially on family occasions like Mothering Sunday. It is a reminder of how costly love can be, and how precious every person is to somebody somewhere.

This gospel story makes the point that every man, woman and child is precious to God no matter what they have done – but it goes further. It is significant that the father insisted that the community come together to celebrate the return of the one who had been missing, highlighting the fact that each individual, no matter what he or she has done, is a member of the human family with rights and entitlements. Sadly, this is by no means as universally accepted as it should be.

There is a tendency to assume that slavery was abolished, yet we still read about the trafficking of millions of people, including young children – exactly what John Newton was doing two centuries ago. Addressing an audience in England in 1999 Archbishop Desmond Tutu said: 'Slavery ... I didn't know about all these forms that existed. I think it's largely because we aren't expecting it. It is hidden. Generally people would not believe that it is possible under modern conditions. They would say, "No, I think you are making it all up," because it is just too incredible.' However, a recent report suggests that over 180 million children are engaged today in the worst forms of slave labour. They are bought and sold within and across national borders; they often do not have contact with their families and are left to the mercy of ruthless employers. Slavery is only one example of how vulnerable people can be excluded and, worst of all, forgotten.

It is tempting to interpret the story of the Prodigal Son only as a personal, reassuring message: that no matter how we have failed, God is always willing to welcome us. But the story has a wider application too with its emphasis on social responsibility and the right of all to be treated decently and, where appropriate welcomed and rehabilitated. John Newton, who once refused an honorary doctorate saying that the coast of Africa had been his university and that he would never accept a diploma 'except from the poor blacks', only discovered his own worth when he came to respect and recognise the worth of those he had once despised and abused.

If the Christian tries to spread the good news of salvation through Jesus Christ, he should also join in the fight against social injustice and political oppression.

(John Stott)

The Way Of The World

Palm Sunday is much more than a commemoration of a past event.
Together with what followed in that first Holy Week, it is a reminder that
the world always tries to take charge.

Published 31 March 2007

Palm Sunday marks the beginning of the most important week in
the Christian calendar, one that is observed by solemn liturgical
events in churches far and wide. It is tempting to look back to the
events of the first Holy Week and pass judgment on those involved:
those fickle crowds cheering Jesus at first, rejecting him a few days
later; the religious and political leaders of the time apparently more
preoccupied with their own survival than anything else; the friends
and followers of Jesus who failed so miserably due to their betrayal,
denial and desertion. The only sign of hope on the human side was
the loyalty of the women and John, who were there until the end.

We cannot, however, leave the matter there; Holy Week is
ongoing. While we tend to focus on the trial of Jesus and the

consequences for him, the truth is that it was humanity that was on trial and found wanting. When Jesus entered Jerusalem on that first Palm Sunday he was welcomed as a national liberator – but he was much more than that. His intention was to show by example the potential of our humanity for good, and how unconditional love can confront evil. His presence there, threatened as he was by petty political and religious intrigue, connects the gospel to real-life, everyday events. Christianity is never about escaping from reality.

But Holy Week reminds us that a characteristic of struggling humanity is the inability to receive and embrace the perfection God wants for us, and thereby to promote and enjoy justice, peace and reconciliation. We are unable to rise above self-interest or other prejudices and are diminished as a result. So, in a real sense Judas did not betray Jesus, he betrayed himself; Peter did not deny Jesus, he denied himself; the remainder did not desert Jesus, they deserted themselves.

Last week, solemn events took place to mark the anniversary of the passing of legislation in England in 1807 to end slavery, a trade that exemplifies human failure of the worst kind, and sadly one in which churches played a prominent role. In 1963 the struggle in America was still ongoing. Dr Martin Luther King was in prison following a civil rights march. In *Letter from a Birmingham Jail* he responded to local church leaders who had criticised the event and his part in it. He wrote that the biggest stumbling block for freedom was 'the white moderate who is more devoted to 'order' than to justice; who prefers a negative peace which is the absence of tension to a positive peace which is the presence of justice.'

That same attitude was very clearly present in the mind of Pilate and the others who confronted and tried to destroy Jesus. Responding to an accusation that he was an extremist, Dr King declared that Jesus was an extremist for love, citing the command to love our enemies and to bless those that curse us. He insisted that the real choice is between being an extremist for hate or an extremist for love – two emotions powerfully present in the events of Holy Week.

In our reflections this Holy Week, it is important to make the connection between what happened then and what is going on around us today. We know from experience how costly and destructive hatred will always be; it is well documented in the pages of human history. But this is a week made special, not by hatred or betrayal, but by a love that was indestructible and forgiving. It is a love that still, two thousand years on, encourages us to live in hope for our world and for ourselves.

The Cross is a way of life; the way of love meeting all hate with love, all evil with good, all negatives with positives.

(Rufus Moseley)

Stephen Street, Dublin 2

A story in a street name.

Published 13 October 2007

A short distance beyond Dublin's Gaiety Theatre lies a street with a name that tells a story. According to McCready's *Dublin Street Names* (1892), St Stephen's Street, like nearby St Stephen's Green, is named after 'St Stephen's Church 1224–1639 originally the chapel of a Leper Hospital, situated near where Mercer's Hospital now stands'.

We associate leprosy with faraway places, yet it was actually prevalent in Europe for centuries, possibly imported by returning crusaders. It is likely that the term included various diseases, but, whatever the exact condition, people were terrified of becoming infected. In his talks on old Dublin, Éamonn MacThomáis used to say that the origin of the expression to not touch something 'with a forty-foot barge pole' had to do with keeping a safe distance from a leper. True or not, this observation certainly underlines the dread that people had of leprosy.

This provides an interesting background to Luke's Gospel (17:11–19), which tells us about the encounter between Jesus and ten lepers. The men, 'keeping their distance called out saying, "Jesus, Master, have mercy on us!"' and they were healed. But only one returned to give thanks 'and he was a Samaritan'. There were no preconditions and no exclusion zones in the ministry of Jesus; fellow Jew or hated Samaritan, grateful or ungrateful, all had one thing in common: they were sick and needed help.

For centuries lepers were subject to strict control. It is said that in the early Church some were excluded by a symbolic burial, as if they had died; all were forbidden to enter churches or other public places. But the teaching of Jesus demanded more. A spectacular example was the work of Father Damien of Molokai. Molokai is a Hawaiian island that was a place of refuge for hundreds of leprosy sufferers in the nineteenth century. Father Damien volunteered to go there to care for the people, including children, and as well as serving them as priest took on the role of doctor and nurse. Sadly, he contracted the disease himself and died in 1889, aged forty-nine. Today in many religious and other organisations Father Damien has been adopted as the model of how society should treat HIV/AIDS patients, for he reminds us that with Jesus those perceived to be untouchable become touchable.

We live in an age of religious cynicism when the failures of the Church are often highlighted. But it is important to acknowledge the good things in our everyday lives that are rooted in the efforts of people trying to live the Jesus way. In his poem 'The Moon in the Lleyn', the Anglican priest R.S. Thomas reminds us of the sacred ever-present within the secular: 'Religion is over, and what will emerge from the body of the new moon, no one can say. But a voice sounds in my ear: Why so fast mortal? These very seas are baptised. The parish has a saint's name time cannot unfrock. In cities that have outgrown their promise people are becoming pilgrims again, if not to this place then to the recreation of it in their own spirits.' What Father Thomas is telling us here is that although the circumstances of ministry may change, the needs and the opportunities for service remain.

We see an example of this in Ireland's work among leprosy victims, and particularly in the work of Wellesley C. Bailey. Bailey came across victims of the disease while teaching in India in 1869. He was deeply distressed by their plight and after several years working in a leper colony returned home to Dublin to tell friends about the desperate need of these people. He raised money, but more importantly he encouraged others to join him in this work, for 'God had taken the lead and that we must follow'. Bailey and his friends had started what is now known as the Leprosy Mission, a worldwide, interdenominational Christian organisation working in many countries. And all this and more, because the Man from Galilee taught us that no one is ever beyond the reach of God's love and care. Not even those who forget to say 'thank you'.

Learn from yesterday, live for today, hope for tomorrow.
(Albert Einstein)

Blessed Assurance

Whether we believe in God or not is a matter of opinion. God's belief in us, however, is never in question.

Published 15 September 2007

We spend a great deal of time discussing whether or not we believe in God. The Gospel of St Luke (15:1–10) reminds us though that God never stops believing in any of us. Jesus, criticised by the religious people around him for 'welcoming sinners' responds by telling them the parables of the lost coin and the lost sheep and the celebrations that followed their recovery. 'I tell you there will be more joy in heaven over one sinner who repents than over ninety-nine righteous people who need no repentance.' At first reading who could disagree? It seems reasonable in principle that those who fail should have the opportunity to make a fresh start. Difficulties arise, however, when we consider the practical implications. Is this available to everyone who repents irrespective of what they have done? Experience would suggest that at a human level many would not be comfortable with that idea. Abraham Lincoln's advice that 'mercy bears richer fruits than strict justice' would not win many votes in today's world.

In Britain in 1966 Myra Hindley together with Ian Brady, was found guilty of the infamous Moors murders in which five children were kidnapped, tortured and killed.

The judge who sentenced them to life imprisonment described Brady as 'wicked beyond belief' and 'beyond hope of redemption'. When one considers the awfulness of their crimes it is hard to disagree. In time Brady was transferred to a secure psychiatric unit. Hindley made many strenuous efforts to gain her freedom. She made at least two attempts to escape and lodged several appeals but all to no avail. Her hopes were finally dashed when the British government, with strong public support, announced that both she and Brady would never be released. She died in prison in 2002.

While in prison Hindley claimed to have recovered her Christian faith and soon gained the support of the late Lord Longford and others who campaigned for her release. Their efforts were backed up by prison officials and the parole board who were convinced that she was genuinely repentant and no longer a danger to society. But the families of the victims and the public at large felt differently. To them, she, like Brady, 'was beyond redemption' and anyone who disagreed was dismissed as a 'do-gooder'. It is reported that none of her family, not even her mother, was present at her funeral. One woman who did attend left a note which read 'Burn in Hell'.

Many, like that woman, find it difficult to accept that in God's world if Hindley's repentance was genuine then she and others like her deserve reinstatement and restoration, no matter how foul their deeds. We find it difficult to comprehend a divine love that is so forgiving. We much prefer to confine these parables of the lost coin and the lost sheep to some vague religious domain, and to conceal their significance as universal gospel truths with implications for everyone without exception. The message is that God actively seeks us out no matter what we have done or how we have failed. St Paul knew this from personal experience: 'I am grateful to Christ Jesus our Lord ... because he judged me faithful and appointed me to his service even though I was formerly a blasphemer, and persecutor and a man of violence' (1 Timothy 1:12). We forget too easily that this great man had a violent and cruel past.

In the Ireland of today with the genuine concerns about crime, especially violent crime and its unfortunate victims, it is understandable that people demand a retributive justice system with ever harsher punishments. However, others argue for a restorative justice system, in which there is accountability for the wrong done, real attention to the needs of the victim and others involved, and an acceptance of the offender's potential for rehabilitation. There may be little support for this approach, but gospel teaching suggests that it is much closer to the Christian understanding of how things are in God's world.

> *The perfection of justice implies charity, because we have a right to be loved.*
>
> *(Austin O'Malley)*

Who Cares?

In 2007, the body of a homeless man was found crushed to death in a Limerick waste disposal facility. It placed the issue of homelessness and poverty once again on the public agenda.

Published 29 September 2007

The grim headline 'Man crushed to death while sleeping in a wheelie bin' was followed by details of the recent tragic death of a homeless man in Limerick. It made for uncomfortable reading. The plight of homeless people is clear to anyone walking the streets of our cities. We encounter it in those outstretched hands that silently ask for help – and we don't quite know what to do. Sometimes we pretend not to see and walk on, or offer some small help hoping it will be well used. And sometimes we dismiss such people as undeserving, even though we know little or nothing about them.

Gavin Bryars, the English composer, tells of 'a tramp' he met while working on a film about homeless people in London. The man wandered the streets singing a song, 'Jesus' blood never failed me yet'. Bryars was struck not only by his faith but also by the quality of his voice. He improvised a simple accompaniment for a recording which had been made of the old man singing. When it was heard by students at the college where he taught, he was amazed at the reaction: 'I found that normally lively room unnaturally subdued. People were moving about much more slowly ... and a few were sitting alone, quietly weeping. This convinced me of the emotional power of the music ... which respected the tramp's nobility and simple faith.' The recording was later published, but sadly the old man did not live to hear it.

Our responsibility to people on the margins is emphasised in St Luke's Gospel (16:19–31) which is about a rich man 'dressed in purple and fine linen and who feasted sumptuously every day'. At his gate, a poor man, Lazarus, lay sick and hungry – and ignored. The dogs were kinder to Lazarus than his affluent neighbour, who was totally indifferent. This parable exposes a false distinction that is sometimes made between the spiritual gospel and the social gospel. The spiritual enables us to develop an intimacy with God by giving us a sense of purpose and direction in our lives. But part of that direction is our responsibility for each other as human beings. St John is specific: 'If anyone has the world's goods and sees his brother in need, yet closes his heart against him, how does God's love abide in him?' (1 John 3:17) Indifference to those in need is not an option – there is no such thing as privatised Christianity.

We need to listen to people on the margins if we are to address their real needs. Thora Mackey of UNICEF, speaking at a school prize-giving, told of a visit she made to a family in rural South Africa. The father had died of an AIDS-related illness some years previously, and the mother had just recently passed away. The eldest child, a girl of seventeen, was left with the responsibility of looking after her younger siblings. Ms Mackey told her audience: 'Just before we got up to leave, I asked her was there anything she wanted. I expected her to say something like more food, some blankets, cooking utensils, clothes – any one of the basic necessities they were without. She thought for a while and then asked shyly if there was any way we could make sure that she got to go into her final year in school. Her mother had always taken care of it and now she was afraid she wouldn't be able to go back to finish her studies.' When we engage with people we discover their real needs.

A prayer traditionally attributed to St Francis of Assisi makes the point that when we focus on the needs of others we ourselves are enriched. We discover qualities and gifts within ourselves which may surprise us but will certainly make us feel better about ourselves.

> *For it is by giving that we receive; it is by losing that we find;*
> *it is by forgiving that we are forgiven; and it is by dying that*
> *we rise again to eternal life.*
>
> (St Francis)

A Mother's Love

The face of human love. A thought for Mothering Sunday.

Published 2 March 2008

One of the world's great religious sculptures is the *Pietà* by Michelangelo that stands in St Peter's Basilica in Rome. The *Pietà* was traditionally a work of art, usually a sculpture, depicting a grief-stricken Virgin Mary holding the dead body of Jesus in her arms. Michelangelo gives us something quite different, however, in that Mary's face is calm and serene reflecting perhaps the Christian confidence that the sufferings of life can be mitigated, and that death is not the final event. This work is a statement of hope with an Easter dimension.

It is said that Michelangelo was criticised for representing Mary as a young woman given that she would have been middle-aged at the time of the crucifixion. He responded by saying first of all that he considered her to be ageless, unaffected by the passage of time. But secondly and interestingly he said that he was also thinking of his own mother who had died when he was only five years old, leaving him to grow up in an all-male household where there was little affection. The intimacy and the closeness of mother and son in his *Pietà* is influenced by his love for his own mother and the pain of her loss which he still felt when he created this masterpiece at the age of twenty-four.

Mothering Sunday is an occasion to celebrate family life, and in particular the role of women. In St John's Gospel we are reminded, however, that religion can easily get it wrong when it comes to dealing with family issues and relationships. Jesus heals a man who was 'blind from birth'. The reaction of the disciples is fascinating. They assume that the man or his parents were in some way responsible for his condition, and ask Jesus which of them had sinned. In doing so, they were reflecting the standard Old Testament teaching on the subject. Where they could only see a theological problem, Jesus saw a human problem, an opportunity to show God's love in action, and responded accordingly. This is an important point for those parents who have the extra responsibility of caring for children with special needs. The 'whys' and the 'wherefores' are beyond us; the selfless love they give is the reality that moves us all.

After the questioning disciples come the Pharisees. They are blinded by their hatred of Jesus and unable to see any good in what has taken place. They suggest that the healing is a set-up; that the man was never blind. Frustrated on that point, they try to turn the man against Jesus, whom they describe as a sinner because he heals on the Sabbath. But the man refuses; all he knows is that he was once blind and now can see. Frustrated yet again the Pharisees resort to the we-know-best position – they are disciples of Moses and therefore they cannot be questioned.

The reality is that these most religious of men feel threatened by the Jesus approach to things. Preoccupied with the threat to their own power and influence, they have lost sight of a human tragedy made good. They cannot cope with the possibility that they are being pointed beyond themselves to something better.

Churches, like the Pharisees of old, can sometimes felt threatened when faced with new theological insights or changing social patterns. It is painful to recall, for example, the damage done to family life and the bitterness caused over many years in this country by official Church attitudes to inter-church marriages. The love, which was God's gift to two people, was made subject to denominational interests. Some families suffer to this day as a result, and must wonder what it was all about.

We are reminded by Michelangelo's *Pietà* that the cross of Jesus has a very human side to it. The personal dimension, his love for his own mother, reminds us that human relationships do matter, that love is the greatest gift of all – and the costliest.

> *Love is the greatest of all risks … the giving of myself.*
>
> (Jean Vanier)

Kristallnacht

Kristallnacht: the ever-present past.

Published 8 November 2008

On 9 November 1938 an infamous campaign of terror was launched against German Jews. What became known as Kristallnacht was reported the next day in the *New York Times* as follows: 'A wave of destruction and looting swept over Germany as National Socialist cohorts took vengeance on Jewish shops, offices and synagogues. Huge, mostly silent crowds looked on and the police confined themselves to regulating traffic.'

In the years since, the world has united to condemn these atrocities. Churches, in particular, have been anxious to distance themselves from responsibility; however, it is arguable that Kristallnacht may well have had its origins in the history of Christian Europe. Without centuries of Christian anti-Semitism, it is questionable whether Hitler's hatred, expressed in *Mein Kampf*, could have taken root. He wrote: 'Was there any shady undertaking, any form

68

of foulness, especially in cultural life in which at least one Jew did not participate?'

The Dutch Theologian, Henri Nouwen, suggests that our present emotions are dependent on memory. 'Remorse is a biting memory, guilt is an accusing memory, gratitude is a joyful memory and all such emotions are deeply influenced by the way we have integrated past events into our way of being in the world.' This suggests that we cannot ignore the past, no matter how hard we try. In a real sense, recognised or unrecognised, the past shapes the present and the future.

The late Archbishop Robert Runcie, who as a young soldier was one of the first to enter the Belsen concentration camp said, 'The travesty of Kristallnacht and all that followed is that so much was perpetrated in Christ's name. To glorify the Third Reich, the Christian faith was betrayed. The slaughter of the Jews was a desecration of the ministry of Jesus, himself a Jew.' And this was done to a people whose genius had enriched and inspired the human race for centuries and who, for Christians, are the people of God who gave us the Hebrew Scriptures and so much of our heritage of faith. This awareness compounds the awfulness of their betrayal.

So what lessons are to be learned from this tragedy of not so long ago? Firstly, there is the possibility that behind our blind prejudices, there may well be the justification for another's violent and hateful action. The silent crowds mentioned in that *New York Times* report were not all innocent bystanders – and many would probably have claimed to be Christian.

For Christians, there is also the painful reminder that Kristallnacht was another example of institutional religion placing its own interests above gospel obligations. We rightly honour Christians who have suffered because of their commitment to the faith, but we rarely think of those within the Church and outside it who have suffered because Christians were unable to live by what they preached. The prophet Amos conveys this blunt message to the Church: 'I hate, I despise your festivals, and I take no delight in your solemn assemblies ... Take away from me the noise of your songs; to the melody of your harps I will not listen. But let justice roll down like waters, and righteousness like an ever-flowing stream.' (Amos 5:21 ff)

One of the amazing features of the Christian story is that no matter how often the Church fails, God is never without witnesses. Maria Skobtsova was a Russian Orthodox nun living in Paris in the early twentieth century. For her, unconditional hospitality and love of one's neighbour were the foundation of the Christian gospel. She used a rented house as her convent. It was a place with an open door for refugees and the needy and when the Nazis entered Paris Jews soon came seeking help and shelter. Mother Maria was eventually exposed and arrested by the Gestapo. She was sent to the camp in Ravensbrück, Germany where on Holy Saturday, 1945, she was sent to the gas chamber – taking the place of someone else.

The tyrant dies and his rule ends; the martyr dies and his rule begins.

(Søren Kierkegaard)

Whose We Are

Love – a many splendored thing.

Published 25 October 2008

Love, according to St Thérèse of Lisieux, 'is the vocation which includes all others; it's a universe of its own, comprising all time and space – it's eternal.' This is the core message in St Matthew 22:39 where we are told that as well as loving God we must also love our neighbour as ourselves. The neighbour is not just that friendly person living next door or across the road but anyone who is in trouble or in need. The parable of the Good Samaritan leaves us in no doubt on that point. Experience shows, however, that we are experts when it comes to moderating its challenging demands when it suits us.

It is important to recognise that love understood in these terms is a powerful and dynamic force for good in the world. Almost forty years ago in Northern Ireland, an ecumenical group from the main churches met to seek a solution to the catastrophe that was unfolding all around them. One young person, a student, said, 'It's simple: love your neighbour as yourselves.' Sadly, for many in Northern Ireland, that was not an option, and a terrible price is still being paid for that failure. But it is not a failure peculiar to Northern Ireland; it is a basic flaw in the human character which opens the door not only to sectarianism and bigotry, but also to racism and a whole range of social injustices. Consider, for example, the status of the travelling community whose children's educational needs have been targeted in the recent budget. Will anyone march for them? While there have been heroic efforts made on their behalf in the past, led mainly by religious orders, many find it difficult to be to them what Christ calls us to be because we cannot bear the cost socially or materially.

We are to love our neighbours as ourselves. Loving ourselves is not as easy as we might think. Some, conscious of past failures or personal inadequacies, may feel unworthy. Others will perhaps think that there is an element of smugness, or even a lack of humility in doing so. But loving oneself in the Christian understanding is not about self-adulation or pretending to be something we aren't. It has nothing to with personal achievement. We are to love ourselves because we are made in the image of God; our lives are part of God's gift to creation and each one of us is an absolutely unique and gifted individual. This is demonstrated in the way Jesus honoured all people, even those who had failed terribly. For him everyone deserved to be valued and respected, and he underlined their individuality by telling them that even the hairs on their heads were numbered. Modern science has taken us much further with the discovery of fingerprinting, voice printing and of course DNA. When the psalmist reflected long ago that he was 'fearfully and wonderfully made', little did he realise just how wonderful.

We live in a world of different values where self-esteem is easily undermined by expectations that are imposed by commercial and other interests. We are often judged by who we are or how we look.

A well-known cosmetic firm encourages people to buy its products with the slogan 'because you're worth it'. There is nothing wrong with people taking care of their appearance; indeed it is important to feel good about oneself, but the Christian gospel tells us we are worth much more and for far better reasons. It tells us we are special no matter how humble our job or how modest our lifestyle; that we have something to contribute whatever our age or experience; that we are valued as human beings whatever our race or religion. We are told to love ourselves not because of *who* we are, but because of *whose* we are: none other than God, who is love.

Love is the greatest thing that God can give us; for himself is love: and it is the greatest thing we can give God; for it will also give ourselves, and carry with it all that is ours.

(Jeremy Taylor)

St Patrick's Day

The Wearin' of the Green.

Published 15 March 2008

This is a weekend for processions and parades. On St Patrick's Day, people at home and abroad will celebrate what it means to them to be Irish. It is worth remembering though that it is a saint's day – a holy day – when we ought to give thanks to God for those who brought the Christian faith to this part of the world. This fact is sometimes overlooked in a sea of political and commercial influence. It is interesting to note recent comments by President Sarkozy of France: 'I consider that a nation which does not know the ethical, spiritual and religious heritage of its history, commits a crime against its culture.'

On Palm Sunday, Christians recall a different parade – the entry of Jesus into Jerusalem. The crowds who cheered Jesus that day were as proud of their identity as Jews as we are of being Irish. But they were a captive people in their own country and longed to be free of Roman rule. For them, Jesus had the potential to be the promised one who would re-establish them as a free and separate people. This longing to be different, separate, was deeply embedded in their consciousness and was not confined to politics; after all, they were the chosen people. Their distinctiveness was affirmed by laws and customs that kept outside influences at bay and imposed social and religious structures within. In the Temple, for example, separation was institutional and physical – Gentile from Jew; men from women; and priest from people.

Citing this in his recent book *Life Conquers Death,* John Arnold, former Dean of Durham, observes that the religion of Jesus' day 'was characterised by the concept of separation' from earliest times. On the other hand he argues that Jesus from the very beginning was the opposite, refusing to be constrained by barriers of any kind: 'He begins life on earth ... with a birth which appears to transgress the bounds of decency, legitimacy and biology.' Dr Arnold gives examples from the ministry of Jesus to illustrate the point: how, for example, he touches a leper in the course of a healing event, thus breaking a strict and sensible hygiene rule. He causes uproar by eating with tax collectors and sinners, ruthless types, engaged in crime and treachery and calls one of them to be a disciple. He helps Roman soldiers and speaks well of the hated Samaritans. In the course of the Last Supper, Jesus washes the disciples' feet, 'consciously doing work which was reserved for women, slaves and gentiles, crossing over to them, identifying himself with these separated fellow human beings subjected as it were to primitive forms of apartheid.' In effect, this Jesus, this 'Man for Others', who ignored man-made boundaries – social, political and religious – could never have fulfilled the expectations of that first Palm Sunday crowd. Good Friday was inevitable because he refused to become the private property of any nation or religion.

It is easy to look back and criticise those who misunderstood Jesus at that time and brutally rejected him within days; however, it is more important to consider to what extent do we misunderstand or misrepresent him today.

During Holy Week we will again contemplate the cross as a way of life; the way of meeting hate with love and evil with good. This is only possible when we cross barriers and reach beyond ourselves to love the unlovable, to touch the untouchable, to forgive the unforgivable and to reach the unreachable. These are the very qualities that brought St Patrick to our shores. Let's not remember him by forgetting what he was about.

> *Love for one's country which is not part of one's love for humanity is not love, but idolatrous worship.*
>
> *(Erich Fromm)*

What It Means To Be Free

Forgiveness was a real force in the early days of South Africa's new-found freedom.

Published 13 September 2008

When Nelson Mandela was freed from prison in 1990 at the age of seventy-one, he had served twenty-seven years of a life sentence, much of it in hard labour on Robben Island near Cape Town. The world has since come to love and respect this great human being because of his lack of bitterness and his determination to work for a new South Africa, one that is at peace with itself. Henry Kissinger, the American statesman, described Mandela as a great leader because he was 'someone who could lead his people to a place where they have not been'. He was referring to Mandela's success in turning his people away from violence to seek peace and reconciliation with those they had once considered their enemies.

A critical component of that change was Mandela's awareness of the power of forgiveness. In several speeches after his release, he astonished audiences with his emphasis on the need to forgive: 'We especially should learn to forgive each other because when you intend to forgive you heal part of the pain, but when you forgive, you heal completely. As Africans we have suffered in terms of slavery and colonialism for a very long time. Forgiveness has remained our best cultural heritage.' Nelson Mandela has given the world proof that forgiveness, a core Christian principle, makes sense and works. It worked for him personally and it worked for his country. It could do wonders for this country with its too-long memory of past injustices. The late Jacqueline Kennedy once asked a friend why the Irish always seemed to consider themselves only as victims.

There are several examples in the teaching of Jesus to show that he believed that forgiveness was a defining characteristic of our relationship with God and with each other. In the Gospel of St Matthew (18:21) Peter raises the subject: 'How often should I forgive? As many as seven times?' Peter was being generous here because at that time many would have held that to forgive someone three or four times was sufficient. But Jesus goes further – much, much further – and tells Peter there can be no limit: 'Not seven times but seventy times seven.'

In the Lord's Prayer Jesus taught us to pray for forgiveness: 'Forgive us our trespasses as we forgive those who trespass against us.' These words are so familiar to us that we often overlook the truth that William Temple reminds us of – 'only one petition in the Lord's Prayer has any condition attached to it; it is the petition for forgiveness.' This implies that when we say 'as we forgive' we take our own salvation into our hands, because whatever God does in this respect depends on what we do. If we cannot forgive we will not be forgiven, because unconditional love is a basic requirement of what it means to be a Christian.

We have all been hurt at some time in our lives, and probably have been instrumental in hurting others as well. When we are wronged it is often easier to retire in self-pity or anger than to find a way to deal with the situation. This is because our instinct is to retaliate or to punish in the mistaken belief that to forgive is to condone. But forgiveness does not condone what is wrong, nor does it mean 'forgetting' what has been said or done. Rather, it means no longer allowing the offence to make a difference or to control our actions.

Archbishop Desmond Tutu, that other great South African, offers this advice: 'When I talk of forgiveness I mean the belief that you can come out the other side a better person. A better person than the one being consumed by anger and hatred. Remaining in that state locks you in a state of victimhood, making you almost dependent on the perpetrator. If you can find it in yourself to forgive then you are no longer chained to the perpetrator. You can move on, and you can even help the perpetrator to become a better person too.'

A Reasonable Hope

Two thousand years on, the Easter story still offers hope in a world of much pain and suffering.

Published 11 April 2009

It is important when discussing Easter to bear two things in mind. First of all, the priority should be to seek the truth rather than try to win an argument. Secondly, one must realise that Christian theology has never claimed that the fact of the resurrection could be known as distinct from faith. The New Testament witnesses had great difficulty understanding or making sense of it, as many still do today. It was important for them to ask questions and the same applies to us; it is essential if we are to have an informed faith.

There is no account in the gospels of the resurrection itself – all the disciples knew was that late on Good Friday Jesus was dead and buried and early on Easter morning the tomb was empty. The first visitors to the tomb that we know of were women who went there to anoint a dead body. They had no expectations beyond that and were disturbed and frightened by what they found. Soon, others were on the scene, and word spread that something very strange had occurred. Not only had the body gone – and that was distressful in itself – but several of those involved reported encounters with Jesus. Reactions were mixed: some believed, some were uncertain and some were downright sceptical.

Two important points emerge from these events. The first is that the followers of Jesus came to believe that Jesus was alive and present to them after his death, although in a radically different way. For them he continued to be a figure of the present, not simply of the past. And Christians today share that belief not only because of that brief series of incidents that occurred two thousand years ago, but also because of their own gathered experience of that presence right up to and including our own time.

The second point is that in the resurrection God had vindicated Jesus. He had said 'Yes' to Jesus and 'No' to those who wanted to destroy him.

If we focus only on Good Friday we are left with a cynical and despairing view of life which suggests that what occurred that day was the final word; that the ruthless and the powerful will always be in control and that the weak and vulnerable will always lose. Furthermore, it means that Christianity belongs to the next world, if it belongs anywhere.

Easter is the reversal of all that. It is a clear declaration that nothing will be allowed to frustrate God's will and loving purpose. Because of Easter, St Paul expressed the firm conviction that nothing in all creation – not even life or death – could separate us 'from the love of God which is in Christ Jesus our Lord'. In his book *The Last Week*, Martin Borg reminds us how trust in the God of Easter still frees and enables people to do important things:

> Without this personal centring in God, Dietrich Bon-
> hoeffer would not have had the freedom and the courage

to engage in a conspiracy against Hitler within Nazi Germany itself. Without it Desmond Tutu could not have opposed apartheid with such courage, infectious joy and a reconciling spirit. Without it Martin Luther King could not have kept on in the midst of all the threats that he faced.

Many other names could be added to the list, women and men whose courage and faith encourages us to live in hope for ourselves, for those we love, and for our world.

Easter means hope prevails over despair. Jesus reigns as Lord of Lords and King of Kings … Easter says to us that despite everything to the contrary God's will for us will prevail, love will prevail over hate, justice over injustice, peace over exploitation and bitterness.

(Archbishop Desmond Tutu)

Wanting And Losing

The demise of the Celtic Tiger was more a moral failure than an economic failure.

Published 1 August 2009

In April 1770, the composer Mozart, who was in his early teens at the time, visited Rome with his father. It was Holy Week and they attended ceremonies in St Peter's where for the first time, the young Mozart heard the magnificent *Miserere* by Gregorio Allegri. He was overwhelmed by the music, but it was forbidden, on pain of excommunication, for anyone to copy or perform this piece anywhere else. That did not deter the young Mozart, who quickly returned to his lodgings and wrote down the entire piece from memory – an extraordinary feat by any standard.

It is important not to let the music, however wonderful, obscure the words of Psalm 51 which it accompanies. It begins: 'Have mercy upon me O God [*Miserere mei, Deus*].'

Historically, this psalm may have been used as an acknow-ledgement of corporate responsibility for the nation's failures by the people (led by their rulers). It begins with a fervent prayer for mercy, making the point that their ultimate failure was moral; the essence of this failure was that it was a rejection of God's will, even though others suffer as a result: 'Against you only have I sinned and done what is evil in your sight.' There is a strong tradition in the Old Testament of calling the nation to account in this way, for these were a people who, on the face of it, gave religion a prominent place in their lives. Again and again, although they were good at what might be called the religious externals, the rituals and so on, they failed to live what they professed in worship, especially when it came to economic and social justice.

As a people, we Irish have been too confident about our religious virtue for too long. We put enormous efforts into religious observance, but if we consider the state of the nation today – and indeed the state of the Church – are there not serious question marks over the integrity of it all?

In the current economic crisis, for example, it is understandable that people are angry with those in positions of influence, such as politicians and bankers. Yet, doesn't responsibility extend much further? To those of us who indulged in waste and excess? We wanted and voted for more and more and more. As our human instincts to be selfish and greedy took over, we supported those who promised us most with little regard for the consequences for the country and no thought for those who were given least. Ours is a moral crisis with economic consequences – a failure to live responsibly as a nation in the light of the values to which we have long paid lip service. And our response as a people is fragmented, pointing fingers everywhere but at ourselves. There is little sign of the corporate sense of guilt or responsibility represented in the psalm.

There is nothing new in this. St Jerome, for one, was aware of similar problems back in the fourth century:

> To our shame, the world is tumbling down in ruins all round us, but our sins are not included in the downfall. There is no country in the world without its asylum seekers. Buildings once regarded as sacred have fallen in dust and ashes and yet we still set our hearts on value for money. We live as though we were going to die tomorrow, and yet we build houses as though we were going to be here forever. Our walls, entrance porches are lavishly luxurious, while Christ is dying at our doors naked and starving in the persons of his poor.

We make a fundamental error if we think that our problems are purely economic and that money can solve everything. We need to recover things of much greater value, those gospel values which are the bedrock of a just and fair society. A mark of that society will be that the vulnerable and the disadvantaged at home and abroad are protected. Christians must speak up, not for themselves, but for those who are not and will not be heard.

Theirs is an endless road, a hopeless maze, who seek for goods before they seek for God.

(*St Bernard of Clairvaux*)

ᥫᕤ

Faith That Lasts

In 1945 Aidan MacCarthy from Castletownbere was a prisoner of war in Nagasaki, Japan when a nuclear bomb was dropped on that city.

Published 15 August 2009

A Doctor's War is a fascinating account of the wartime experiences of Dr Aidan MacCarthy from Castletownbere in West Cork. A former pupil at Clongowes Wood, he graduated from the Cork Medical School in 1938 and joined the Royal Air Force as a medical officer the following year. He was posted to France but soon found himself on the Dunkirk beaches awaiting evacuation. He was later sent to the Far East, where in 1942 he was taken prisoner by the then all-conquering Japanese. In this book, MacCarthy details the appalling treatment that he and many others received at the hands of their captors. He was eventually moved to a camp in Nagasaki in Japan, where he witnessed the devastation caused by the dropping of the nuclear bomb on that city.

Through these horrors, deprived of every human dignity and material comfort, MacCarthy continued to work as a doctor. He vividly describes one incident where he was attending a dying airman and had no medicine to ease the man's terrible pain: 'All that I could do for him was to pray and to hold his hand and whisper words of encouragement. As I tried to comfort him I wondered if the dying man was able to find strength in faith as I was. I remembered the devoutness of my own upbringing; I remembered our village priest and myself as a child, serving before the altar, and once again I thanked God for the faith that sustained me under these appalling conditions.'

Remarkably, this young doctor who on one level had nothing – everything that could be taken from him had been taken – on a much deeper level had so much to share.

Jesus had no illusions about the difficulties facing his followers in this cruel world, given their vocation to lives of loving service. He knew that for them to maintain such a costly ministry they would require support of a special kind which he described in these words: 'Very truly I tell you, unless you eat the flesh of the Son of Man and drink his blood, you have no life in you' (John 6:53).

It is important to get behind the language to the substance: that the life that Jesus offers is the life of the resurrection, which defeats any fear or injustice, however menacing. This was the experience of Leonard Wilson, who was Anglican bishop of Singapore when the Japanese invaded in 1942. Like Dr MacCarthy, he suffered terribly as a prisoner, yet still managed to minister to his fellow prisoners, often by celebrating the Eucharist using grains of rice and water.

Wilson reflected on his ordeal some years later:

> How easy it is to forget God and all His benefits. I had known Him in a deeper way than I could ever have imagined, but God is to be found in the Resurrection as

well as in the Cross, and it is the Resurrection that has the final word. God was revealed to me, not because I was a special person, but because I was willing in faith to accept what God gave. I know it is true not just because the Bible says so or because the Church has told us, but because I have experienced it myself, and whether you are despondent or in joy, whether you are apathetic or full of enthusiasm, there is available for you at this moment the whole life of God with its victory over sin and pain and death.

The experiences of these two men bring to life words from long ago: 'Who going through the vale of misery, use it for a well: and the pools are filled with water. They will go from strength to strength and unto the God of gods appeareth every one of them in Sion' (Psalm 84:6–7).

Lights Out

Light shines in the darkness and the darkness cannot overcome it. The story of a Jewish poet and mother.

Published 5 December 2009

Ilse Weber, the Jewish poet, writer of children's books and radio producer lived in Prague until 1942 when she, her husband and son, were sent by the Nazis to the local Terezín concentration camp. Ilse worked as a nurse looking after children in the camp until, again with her husband and child, she was sent to Auschwitz in 1944. She and her little boy were later executed; her husband survived the war. Ilse was a fine musician and sometimes entertained her fellow prisoners. It is said that she would sing 'Wiegala', a lullaby she wrote, to soothe anxious children on their way to the gas chambers. Ilse somehow remained dignified in the presence of an obscene evil. She was defiant, determined not to be crushed by the apparent hopelessness of her circumstances.

What is it about the human spirit that so often refuses to give in no matter how bad things seem to be? The Ilse Webers of life are an inspiration and an encouragement when we are tested by the 'changes and chances of this fleeting world'. We are not facing anything like the horrors of wartime but many people in the Ireland of today are being severely tested to the point of despair by what is going on all around them. The gloom of the economic situation is compounded by the terrible flood damage which has destroyed the homes and livelihoods of thousands. The tragic loss of promising young lives in recent road accidents is painfully sad. Worst of all are the latest disclosures about the abuse of children and the deliberate cover-up. We struggle to find meaningful words of explanation or comfort in such circumstances. It is not easy to hope 'in a world which seems empty of God's presence'.

Yet it is the real world we take with us as we journey through Advent towards Christmas with liturgies that urge us to think positively. They abound with images of darkness yielding to light; of despair making way for hope. This sense of hope connects with our human instinct that there is an ultimate goodness overseeing our progress, and that in the end all shall be well, no matter how awful things are now. Some of course find such a hope difficult because it is beyond human resources to deliver and that is understandable. It is one thing to hope for better days; it is quite another to make them happen.

In his book *Priestland's Progress*, Gerald Priestland explains his own faith journey:

> The Christian hope – a combination of responsive faith and responsive love – is, in the end, what makes our pilgrimage possible at all. Knowing that God is vulnerable but indestructible, we know that the journey will be strenuous and full of suffering, but that it is not absurd: that it will bring us to the water's edge in the

end. It seems to me that the journey itself has its own value, for it shows me that I am not alone and that I cannot expect to leapfrog over my fellow pilgrims and arrive at the Celestial City by private plane. Christian faith is the Christian's response to life.

It is important to remember that Christian hope does not come from a human source; it is given. The Advent journey points us to a source beyond ourselves, to the person of Jesus Christ. It is a hope demonstrated in his life, death and resurrection and guaranteed by God. It is a hope that can survive the most awful and testing of times.

The following words were written on the wall of a cellar in Cologne where people were hiding during the Second World War. No one would have blamed the author for cursing their enemies, but instead they left a message of hope and love to inspire generations to come: 'I believe in the sun even when it is not shining. I believe in love even when I cannot feel it. I believe in God even when He is silent.'

cᴂ

Science Meets Religion

James Ussher, an Archbishop who got it wrong. The complex relationship between religion and science.

Published 14 February 2009

In certain editions of what is known as the King James translation of the Bible, the year 4004 BC is given as the date of the Creation. This was the conclusion of James Ussher, noted Irish scholar of the seventeenth century and Archbishop of Armagh from 1625 until 1656. Born in Dublin, he was baptised in the historic St Audoen's Church in Cornmarket. Ussher was not alone in providing a biblical chronology but his was the most widely accepted. Not everyone agreed, however, and by the eighteenth century questions were being raised about his 'young earth' theory.

The greatest challenge would come from the later work of Charles Robert Darwin, the English naturalist, who was born 12 February 1809, exactly two hundred years ago this week. His *Origin of Species*, published in 1859, caused uproar, especially among churchmen of the time who were committed to a literal interpretation of the Genesis account of creation. It is worth noting, however, that theologians of the time 'who had pure and spiritual conceptions of God were not so alarmed'.

Thanks mainly to Darwin, Christians were – in some cases reluctantly – forced to come to terms with discoveries of science that impacted on religious belief. It is arguable that as a result, our understanding of God has been enriched and expanded by what we now know of the scale and complexity of the created order. As one hymn by Isaac Watts puts it, 'Lord how thy wonders are displayed where're I turn mine eye; if I survey the ground I tread or gaze upon the sky.'

An unfortunate consequence of the Darwinian controversy has been the mistaken belief that religious faith and scientific knowledge are incompatible. This view overlooks the distinctive, though complementary, roles of the two disciplines: the one concerned with why things came to be, the other with how they came to be.

One of the better known critics of religion is Richard Dawkins, eminent biologist, popular science writer and convinced atheist. In his book *The God Delusion* (2006) he dismisses religion out of hand. Recently his views have been challenged by Professor Keith Ward, a leading philosopher-theologian, in *Why There Almost Certainly Is a God*, which one professor of physics describes as 'a devastating critique of Richard Dawkins' latest foray beyond his sphere of scientific expertise'. Ward agrees with Dawkins that a key question is this: 'Is intelligent mind an ultimate and irreducible reality? Indeed is it the ultimate nature of reality? Or is mind and consciousness an unforeseen and unintended product of basically material processes of evolution.'

Ward argues that those who believe in God are those for whom the universe is rational and intelligible, and that consciousness is a reality that cannot be explained in purely physical, mechanistic terms. 'They will not be mad or deluded, blindly accepting of any human authority or uncritical passing fashion of human thought. They will be lovers of truth and beauty, and they may feel themselves to be ... beloved of God and sharers in divine immortality.'

That science and religion can cohabit is seen in the distinguished career of John Polkinghorne, Fellow of the Royal Society and Professor of Mathematical Physics at Cambridge University from 1968 to 1979. Polkinghorne resigned from his academic post to train for the ministry of the Church of England and was ordained in 1981. He was a founding member of the Society of Ordained Scientists, as well as the International Society for Science and Religion, of which he was the first President. Clearly, for him science and religion were not mutually exclusive.

Perhaps we are at our best as men and women of faith, and as scientists, when we heed the advice of Albert Schweitzer, theologian, musician, philosopher, and missionary doctor who encouraged us to rejoice in the truth 'wherever we find its lamp burning'. Charles Darwin had the courage and the integrity to do just that, and we should be grateful.

Everyone who is seriously interested in the pursuit of science becomes convinced that a spirit is manifest in the laws of the universe – a spirit vastly superior to man, and one in the face of which our modest powers must feel humble.

(Albert Einstein)

The Gift of Womanhood

The status of women in the Church and the plight of women in the world.
There is still a long way to go in putting these matters right.

Published 7 November 2009

One of the key tasks of the Christian Church is to preach reconciliation. William Barclay suggests that never once is God said to be
reconciled to man; it is always man who needs to be reconciled to
God and that's the difficult part. The tragedy is, however, that the
Church, which is called to be the model of reconciliation, is often its
contradiction, because of a preoccupation with internal matters.

We see this in the current debate within the churches about the
role of women in the Church. While there has been a general
acceptance within Anglicanism of women serving in the ordained
ministry, there are those who feel that they cannot accept this break
with tradition, especially where it leads to the ordination of women
bishops.

In response to the situation within Anglicanism Pope Benedict XVI has approved a canonical structure which will allow former Anglicans to enter full communion with the Roman Catholic Church while preserving elements of their distinctive Anglican heritage.

The suggestion that the Archbishop of Canterbury, Dr Rowan Williams, was only informed of this proposal at the last minute has caused disquiet in Anglican circles and beyond. Archbishop George Carey, his predecessor, was 'appalled' that Archbishop Williams only learned of Rome's intention shortly before it was announced: 'I think in this day and age, it was inexcusable to do this without consultation.' The Catholic theologian Father Hans Kung described the offer as a 'tragedy, a non-ecumenical piracy of priests'. These are difficult times for ecumenism.

But what does this tell us about the state of the Church when the role of women within the Church can cause such dissension while the exploitation and abuse of women worldwide goes largely unnoticed? Has Christianity lost its way? The Korean theologian Chung Hyun Kyung speaks of the overwhelming suffering and injustice in the lives of Asian women: 'Female children generally are more poorly fed, less educated and overworked when compared with male children. Even after they grow up, women's lives only get worse under oppressive public and domestic structures ... Their bodies are controlled and their labours are exploited. In their brokenness and longing for a full humanity, Asian women have met and come to know God.' The abuse and exploitation of women and young girls is by no means confined to Asia.

We need to hear what the Spirit is saying to the churches in St Luke's Gospel (20:46) where Jesus comments on the exploitation of women by men in high places: 'Beware of the scribes, who like to walk around in long robes, and to be greeted with respect in the market places and to have the best seats in the synagogues. They devour widows' houses and for the sake of appearance say long prayers.'

He then commends a widow for her generosity, insisting that her contribution is greater than anyone else's – including the men who make the rules. And he said these things in a culture where men praised God daily 'who did not make me a woman'. In a reflection, Sister Virginia Fabella reminds us of the special relationship between Jesus and Mary Magdalene:

> In the social setting of her time, women were 'non-persons' who 'belonged' to some male individual, with no rights of their own. And yet Jesus showed respect for Mary's personhood by calling her by name [in the Easter garden] and gave recognition of her personal dignity as a woman, thus dignifying womanhood as well. There is something significant in the fact that Jesus appreciated Mary's worth for who she was as a person, and not because she was the 'wife of' or 'mother of' or 'daughter of' a superior male. She was Mary of Magdala. Jesus not only recognised her value as a person but ... confirmed her trustworthiness and capability above his other disciples, to be the first witness to the resurrection.

Mary's unique role as the first recorded witness to the resurrection reminds us that in church life, some things are much more important than others.

In Giving We Receive

Generosity is a gift: Jane and Brendan McKenna proved this when they set up the LauraLynn Children's Hospice in 2001, after losing their two children.

Published 10 October 2009

There is something special about a harvest festival in a country church. The abundance of things, the autumnal colours and scents, the enthusiasm of the people who live close to the land, combine to remind us how much we depend on both the good earth and each other. The city dweller is somewhat distanced from nature by his environment. A friend with an interest in astronomy moved out of Dublin because city lights denied him a clear view of the sky at night, something taken for granted in the country.

Wherever we live, the message of harvest festival is that everything we have has been given to us and is given on trust for the benefit not only of ourselves but of others as well. However, we don't always see it that way. We become attached to what we have and feel threatened at any possibility of losing it. It was reported that an old man had died and left a fortune. 'Not so,' said his neighbour, 'He was taken from it.'

Fr John Dalrymple, a Scottish parish priest, warns against a preoccupation with material things in his book *Costing Not Less Than Everything*: 'Christians have to be clear where they stand with regard to property and goods. They should not condemn them since they are good things. But they should be ruthless and radical towards the possessive instinct in themselves. If I do not act ruthlessly against my possessiveness, I will be possessed by it. It will lead me and govern me. I will be caught up in an unending spiral of desire ... and soon both my surrender to God and my openness to my neighbour will have been thrown aside.'

The Gospel of St Luke (18:18) deals with this very issue. A young man asks Jesus what he must do to have eternal life. Jesus points to the commandments and the man assures him that he has kept them from his youth up. Then Jesus, seeing that he was well off, told him he lacked one thing: 'Go sell what you have and give the money to the poor.' The young man was shocked and went away grieving, 'for he had many things'. This is not a repudiation of material things – celebrating and appreciating what we have is very much part of the gospel – rather it is a warning against being possessed by what we possess.

Fr Dalrymple suggests that possessiveness can destroy us: 'Perhaps the reason we so often fail to love as we should is not because of a defect of loving in us, but because we are unwilling to conquer our spirit of greed and so, put ourselves before others. This is true of families as well as individuals.'

Given that we all struggle in such matters, it is good to remember that there are people with unselfish gifts of love and generosity. Jane and Brendan McKenna experienced every parent's nightmare – the loss of two children. Their little girl, Laura, died aged four in 1999;

two years later, they lost their other daughter, Lynn, aged fifteen. We cannot begin to measure their pain. However, their losses inspired them to look to the needs of others facing the same awful possibility; so, they launched the LauraLynn Children's Hospice Foundation in 2001. Jane explains: 'While our own situation is very sad, there are many families coping with far worse. Our hope is to help those families out there, whose children have life-limiting and/or life-threatening conditions, and are coping at present with limited support.' In Ireland there are over 1400 children with life-limiting or life-threatening conditions; hopefully LauraLynn House, a hospice for the young, will soon be fully operational and providing necessary support.

Jesus challenged the young man to part with his money for a good cause – but he turned his back on the joy of giving. We are all challenged as Christians to use what is given to us for the good of others as well as ourselves. The LauraLynn story reminds us how worthwhile and how beautiful a thing that can be.

A man there was, though some did count him mad,
The more he cast away, the more he had.

(John Bunyan)

Laborare Est Orare

Praying for someone or something does not mean sitting back and doing nothing. Prayers have responsibilities attached.

Published 24 October 2009

In her book *Cry Pain, Cry Hope,* the Rev. Elizabeth O'Connor gives a disturbing account of her experiences helping out in a Washington night shelter for street women. She describes the women as they arrive with little or no possessions, grateful to be made welcome and glad to get some food and somewhere to sleep safely for the night.

When morning came, however, their mood changed: 'Distraught women – some of them old and sick – could not comprehend why they were once more being "pushed out" into the streets. We, who had received them warmly the night before, were the very ones hurrying them along, benefactors so soon to become enemies.' She tells of one old woman who started to pray, only to be taunted by another woman: '"God don't hear your prayer." The blunt comment

101

made Ms O'Connor think: "Does God hear her prayer? Then I re-membered God is in me and where I am God is. The real question was "Did I hear her prayer?" "What would it mean to hear her prayer?"'

Every Sunday in our churches we pray for 'the sick, the poor and those in trouble'. Elizabeth O'Connor's point is that when we ask God to listen and address those concerns, his response will often come through the loving action and generosity of people – and not always overtly religious people. The selflessness, she points out, is not always easy. The Letter of St James (2:15) is very practical: 'If a brother or sister is ill-clad and in lack of daily food and one of you says to them, "Go in peace be warmed and filled," without giving them the things needed for the body what does it profit?'

Of course one way of dealing with such challenges is to pretend that they don't exist or don't deserve our attention. In St Luke's Gospel (18:35–43) we hear the story of a blind man called Bartimeus who, realising that Jesus was close by, called out for help. The people around Jesus told him to be quiet, but he persisted, and when Jesus heard him he ordered that he be brought to him. Jesus spoke to him, asking, 'What do you want me to do for you?' The blind man said to him, 'My teacher, let me see again.' And we are told he received his sight.

Like the crowd following Jesus that day, it is tempting to keep at a distance those who are likely to upset things, or make demands that we are unwilling – or unable – to meet. Often they are kept at bay because their presence is seen as a threat to our financial or social interests. Then there are others, such as members of the gay community, whose lifestyles challenge us and who are marginalised and even vilified because we just do not want to know. It is unthinkable that Jesus would ever have excluded people the way we do. Indeed, the only ones excluded from his presence were those who excluded themselves, because they hated his openness to every-one who came his way.

Bishop Willie Walsh tells the story of a couple he ministered to who were not formally married but lived together. The woman was a churchgoer but because of her circumstances was not allowed by her church to receive Holy Communion. They discussed various options but the problem remained and the Bishop found himself in some difficulty: 'Did I become the outsider who tells them not to worry about the Church's law and simply to trust that God's love and care for them is greater than any church law? And did I become a further outsider by praying with them and asking God to bless and enrich their love and their union – a union that will always leave them outsiders?'

And then he adds: 'But then Jesus always seemed to have a special care for outsiders – the lepers, the woman accused of committing adultery, Mary of Magdala, the tax collectors and sinners. Indeed by his very association with outsiders Jesus became an outsider himself.'

Man is never nearer the Divine than in his compassionate moments.

(Joseph Hertz)

Saints Alive

In an age when the credibility of the gospel is challenged we can always point to the women and men of faith whose lives reveal its power.

Published 7 August 2010

'Now faith is the assurance of things hoped for, the conviction of things not seen.' So begins that powerful Chapter Eleven from the letter to the Hebrews, which is something of a grand parade of Old Testament greats commended for their faith and their achievements: 'By faith Abraham obeyed when he was called … by faith Isaac invoked future blessings on Jacob and Esau. By faith Jacob when he was dying blessed each of the sons of Joseph' and so on. The writer is reminding us that faith means trusting in God, come what may. It is only faith that enables us to believe that the universe is God-controlled, and that in this context our lives have meaning and purpose.

But the parade does not end on the pages of the New Testament – it is added to generation by generation. The twentieth century has its own list of greats: by faith Dietrich Bonhoeffer stood against the evils of Nazism; by faith Max Kolbe gave his life to save another; by faith Martin Luther King gave his people a vision of racial harmony and justice; by faith Mother Teresa worked tirelessly for the poor and the dying; by faith Archbishop Oscar Romero confronted the abuse of power; by faith Archbishop Desmond Tutu opposed apartheid and led his people towards peace and reconciliation. In an age of cynicism these people not only affirm the power of faith, they also demonstrate how what is best in the human character is brought out when God's will and purposes are accepted. That, of course, is easy to say, but so much more difficult to do.

In his book *Letters from the Desert* Carlo Carretto comments on this passage from Hebrews.

> The friendly night is an image of faith, that gift of God defined as 'The guarantee of the blessings we hope for and proof of the existence of the realities that at present remain unseen' (Hebrews 11:1). I have never found a better metaphor for my relationship with the eternal: I am this point lost in space; the darkness like an irreplaceable friend is faith; the stars God's witness. When my faith was weak all this would have seemed incomprehensible to me. I was afraid as a child is of the night but now I have conquered it and it is mine. The darkness is necessary, the darkness of faith is necessary for God's light is too great. I understand more and more that faith is not a mysterious and cruel trick of a God who hides himself without telling me why, but a necessary veil. My discovery of him takes place gradually, respecting the growth of the divine life in me.

It is important to realise that great heroes of the faith are not born as heroes. Like all of us they grow up in the world of the ordinary and the routine. The testing of faith comes to them as it does for all of us: unannounced, uninvited and probably unwelcome. The psalmist may talk about 'going through the vale of misery and using it for a well'. That may be the case in retrospect, but there are no queues at the entrance to the vale itself.

Testing came the way of the Russian poet Irina Ratushinskaya, who, at the age of twenty-eight, was sentenced to long years of brutal imprisonment under the former Soviet regime. Her crime? Writing poetry.

In 'All as I Asked', a poem which she wrote in the KGB prison in Kiev in January 1983, she demonstrates how her faith gave her the hope and the confidence that one day she would be delivered: '(O Lord, thank you!) … There will be for me / A heaven won by honour, And a cloak beneath my feet.'

Uncomfortable Truths

Speaking about Religion: The Merriman Summer School does the talking,
not the churches.

Published 21 August 2010

This year the annual Merriman Summer School, which is taking
place in Ennis, Co. Clare, has chosen *Faith: Beyond Belief?* as its theme,
with the intention of addressing questions of faith, belief and religion
in Irish culture and society. It is a timely discussion given current
levels of interest and concern in such matters, prompted to some
extent by controversies within the Roman Catholic Church, but by
no means confined to it. While discussions of this kind are to be
welcomed, it is perhaps significant that they are being discussed
outside the institutional churches rather than within and between
them.

There is a painful truth not always accepted by churches at a
leadership level, which is that there is no such thing as a church with
a monopoly of divine wisdom and authority. There is no church that

can settle decisively and forever what God is like or what he wants. Indeed, it is arguable that an institution claiming such powers is in fact claiming to be God.

The records of all our churches highlight the impropriety of such claims, for they are littered with actions and attitudes that are anathema to the God revealed in the Christian gospel. The terrible injustices done in the name of God are a disgrace not only to God but to humanity. And still there is an air of arrogance about and disdain for what others might think or want to share. The attitude sometimes seems to be: we are above and beyond questioning, and what we say and what we do must not be challenged under any circumstances.

There is an example of this in St Luke 13:10–17 where Jesus is condemned from the pulpit for healing a woman on the Sabbath. The leader of the synagogue denounced Jesus to the crowd for breaking the law. Jesus responds by telling them that they were hypocrites because they would break the very same law if it suited them. Incidentally the word translated 'hypocrite' suggests a person wearing a mask, someone we would describe as two-faced. This is only one of several episodes in the gospel narratives where Jesus exposes the inability of institutional religion to live by the costly values and rules of God's kingdom; instead they opt to hold on to rules and regulations that suit themselves.

David Jenkins, theologian and one-time bishop of Durham, was noted for his challenging and occasionally controversial questioning of the religious establishment. He questioned the idea of a God of the Church, which he felt implied that the Church somehow has ownership and possibly control of God. He writes, 'God must be far more than, and at times very distant from, the church or all churches. We worship God, not the church in any shape or form. That was one of the most fundamental reassertions of the Reformation, and it has to be reasserted again and again. This sort of Protestantism is an essential part of Catholic and apostolic faith and practice. Within, under and through this worship of God we thankfully accept that there is a church of God, which he calls, judges, changes and sustains and above all, mercifully and graciously uses. There is a church of God but there is no God of the church. He is the God of the whole earth and mystery of all things. We belong to him but he does not belong to us.'

Bishop Jenkins is suggesting that the churches need to rediscover the theology that clarifies their true status and purpose. The desire to have power and the instinct to dominate and control must give way to a commitment to humble service and unconditional love in action.

The Other Side

'A little help sir ...' What should the Christian response be to the street beggar?

Published 10 July 2010

Many have had the experience of encountering a homeless person on the street and not knowing what to do. There is a twinge of conscience: do we ignore the person and walk by or offer a little help?

Dr Eva Fogelman, a psychologist who lives in New York, understands:

> I cannot walk more than a few blocks without confronting a homeless beggar, face to face. I am inconsistent in opening my purse for this or that dishevelled young man with a cup in his hand asking for money for a cup of coffee, particularly after working a fourteen-hour day. My numbness to the dire social conditions that have led

to the degradation and humiliation of a homeless beggar is a defence against the helplessness I feel in making a real difference in society. Those of us who would like to think of ourselves as basically caring, good, charitable people are amazed at our numbness to the plight of very needy people. Some of us rationalise that poverty, homelessness, and crumbling families are the system's fault for not providing adequate housing and jobs for all its citizens; others blame the victims for their plight; everyone feels helpless about a more comprehensive solution to these social ills.

Dr Fogelman has reason to be troubled. 'Looking at the faces of homeless men in particular, but also women and children triggers thoughts of my father.' Her Jewish father had miraculously escaped a Gestapo mass killing of Jews in 1942 in Ilya in Belarus. He lived rough for months depending on the kindness of strangers: 'No one dared give my father shelter, since those caught harbouring a Jew earned a death sentence for themselves and their entire family. Nevertheless a local farmer sent his children out to the ditch my father dug in the woods, brought him food, took his lice-infested clothes to wash, and brought him ointment to remove the vermin from his head and body.'

Eva Fogelman's experience quickens our understanding of the story of the Good Samaritan (St Luke 10:25–37) told by Jesus to a lawyer who wants to know what he should do to inherit eternal life. He tells Jesus that he knows what the Bible teaches: that he should love God and love his neighbour as himself. Jesus agrees, but the man is not satisfied and asks: 'Who is my neighbour?' The word 'neighbour' in the Greek means someone who is near, while in the Hebrew it means someone that you have an association with. This limited meaning confines the obligation to fellow Jews, thus excluding Samaritans, Romans, and other foreigners. So Jesus tells the parable of the Good Samaritan, in which a man is attacked and injured, to show that our responsibility for those in trouble knows no boundaries of any kind.

In the parable, the first person to pass by the injured man is a priest. Jesus tells how he showed no compassion for the man, passing on the other side of the road so as not to get involved. Love was not a word for him that required action on behalf of someone else. The next person to pass by is a Levite, and he does exactly the same thing: he passed by without showing any concern. The one person who responds positively is the Samaritan – an outsider – one of a people despised by the Jews at that time, and who has come to represent what is best in the human character like those who assisted Eva Fogelman's father.

She said of them: 'While they were flesh-and-blood human beings with strengths and faults, these rare men, women, and children saw people who were in trouble and responded, not to the things that made them different, but to the points of commonality. Their humanitarian response sprang from a core of firmly held inner values, which included an acceptance of people who were different. And central to these beliefs was the conviction that what an individual did, or failed to do, mattered.'

The parable of the Good Samaritan is challenging, because it means accepting that our neighbour is everyone, and especially those in need. Their side of the street is our side of the street, whether we like it or not.

We can do no great things, only small things with great love.
(Mother Teresa)

Prayer Understood

Prayer is not about words – it is about our relationship with God. It means listening as well as speaking.

Published 24 July 2010

One of the most difficult aspects of our religious lives is the maintenance of an active and purposeful prayer life. For some of us prayer is reserved for emergencies, i.e. when things go wrong and we look for help having exhausted all other sources. That, however, is a somewhat limited understanding of what prayer is about. Prayer is best understood in terms of a developing engagement with God, and therefore should take us far beyond asking for things. It is 'a personal relationship rather than a market transaction' which requires time and attention.

God is not restricted by particular methods or techniques of prayer, which have more to do with personal needs and choices, but openness to God is an essential dimension of prayer. Some people have a sense of God speaking to them while they are on the move, walking the dog or cleaning the house. On the first Easter Day two men on the road to Emmaus were slow to realise that they were being spoken to by an unrecognised Jesus. It was only looking back that they realised what had happened: 'Did not our hearts burn within us while he talked to us on the road?' The important thing in any prayer encounter is to be able to say, like the boy Samuel, 'Speak Lord for your servant hears.'

Not all prayers are answered in the way we would like. The broadcaster Alistair Cooke once told of a cardinal who when asked 'Does God always answer prayer?' replied 'Yes, and he sometimes says "No".'

In St Luke's Gospel (11) the disciples ask Jesus to teach them how to pray and he responds with the words of the Lord's Prayer. The first part is concerned with God and begins by addressing him as Father – again teaching us that prayer means relationship. It reminds us that our first duty in prayer is to fix our attention on God and his will. This sets the parameters for the second part when we address the needs of the world. What is striking about this model of prayer is that at no point is it self-centred. When we ask for daily bread, it is not just for ourselves but for the hungry everywhere. When we ask for forgiveness it is not only for ourselves, but for all who fail, and especially those who do not or cannot pray for themselves. This pattern suggests that a healthy and meaningful prayer life takes us far beyond personal needs, although it does not exclude them.

This notion is underlined by Father Adrian Hastings in his book *The Shaping of Prophecy*, which has particular relevance today. He dismisses what he calls privatised religion, and by implication privatised prayer, as ineffectual and meaningless. For him, if prayer is properly understood it is a powerful transforming influence in people's lives:

> Without prayer and its grounding in faith the human
> city and its politics remain irredeemable. Selfishness and

corruption of sectional interests are too strong. But without politics prayer becomes a selfish ego trip, an escape from that burden of secular reality for which every one of us is inherently responsible. A religion of pure spirituality is a privatised religion with a privatised God, and a privatised God cannot or should not exist. God is the God of everything (or he is the God of nothing) but of everything seen through the image of the crucified. Without such a God and without the human prayer that makes us conscious of such a God there can be no absolute critique of evil government and corrupt politics, no tradition of prophecy.

The Lord's Prayer encourages us to approach God with hope and in confidence. The God to whom we pray is not some distant tyrant to be appeased at all costs, rather he is like a loving father who only wants what is best for us and who is interested in every detail of our lives. It encourages us to think of prayer as a privilege, and not as a burden.

The world may doubt the power of prayer but the saints know better.

(Gilbert Shaw)

Speak Up

South Africa's faith: lessons for Ireland. The Saville report provided some comfort for the victims of Derry's Bloody Sunday.

Published 26 June 2010

The eyes of the world have been on South Africa these past few weeks as the drama of the Football World Cup unfolds and fans look forward to the final, which is in two weeks time. It is quite an extraordinary transformation from the days of apartheid, when South Africa was in the news for all the wrong reasons. Fear and violence were the order of the day and many felt that there was little prospect of anything good happening in the foreseeable future.

But that was to underestimate the influence of courageous leaders like Archbishop Desmond Tutu, who insisted that 'we are prisoners of hope'. This could easily have been seen as mere rhetoric, but the fact is that his Christian faith refused to give up even on the darkest day.

The American writer Jim Wallis witnessed this determination when security police forcibly entered St George's Cathedral, Capetown, where Bishop Tutu was preaching at an ecumenical service: 'The incident taught me more about the power of hope than any other moment in my life. Desmond Tutu stopped preaching and just looked at the intruders as they lined the walls of his cathedral wielding writing pads and tape recorders to record whatever he said … threatening him with consequences for any bold prophetic utterances.' The bishop acknowledged their power – 'You are powerful, very powerful' – but then reminded them that he served a higher power than theirs: 'I serve a God who cannot be mocked.' Tutu would not be deterred.

St Luke's Gospel (9:51–62) reminds us of that key moment in the ministry of Jesus when 'he set his face to go to Jerusalem' before that final encounter with church and state which would lead to his rejection and death. Sensing danger, would-be followers began to make excuses and opted out. His response was sharp and to the point: 'No one who puts his hand to the plough and looks back is fit for the kingdom of God.' We cannot escape the challenges of the present and the future by lingering in the past.

That does not mean we cannot learn from the past. This is evident from the positive reaction to the Saville Bloody Sunday report, which has provided some consolation to the families most affected by that awful day. Coming to terms with the truth about our past, both as a nation and as individuals, can be painful, but it can also be a liberating experience, one that allows us to move forward with confidence and hope. And that is where we now need the kind of courageous Christian leadership that we have seen in South Africa.

In December 1999 Nelson Mandela, while addressing an international conference of religious bodies, said: 'This gathering … serves to counter despairing cynicism and calls us to the recognition and reaffirmation of that which is great, generous and caring in the human spirit.'

He pointed out that when he was a child the state made no provision for the education of black children; that it was the churches that bought land and built and equipped schools, employed teachers and paid them. 'Without the church and religious institutions, I would never have been here today. But to appreciate the importance of religion, you have to have been in a South African jail under apartheid where you could see the cruelty of human beings to others in its naked form. It was again religious institutions who gave us hope that one day we would come out of prison.' Desmond Tutu's boundless hope was crowned by Nelson Mandela's amazing capacity to forgive his former enemies despite long years of harsh imprisonment.

At a time when many people may be disillusioned with religion in Ireland – and for understandable reasons – it is worth recalling the potential of the lived gospel, as seen in South Africa, to transform a nation's life. There are still problems to be faced there but there is also hope and a new confidence. At the heart of that gospel is the conviction that despite all evidence to the contrary, God's purpose will prevail, love will triumph over hate, justice over injustice, generosity over greed, peace over exploitation and bitterness. We must never cease to be 'prisoners of hope'.

A Child of God

Being honest with and about ourselves is an essential part of spiritual growth.

Published 6 March 2010

During Lent we consider the human side of our Lord's life as he makes his final journey to Jerusalem, facing many temptations along the way. In the words of Herbert O'Driscoll: 'We follow the human steps of our Lord as he wrestles with his own humanity. We go with him into the wilderness where both he and we must try to find the right path if we are to respond to God's will for us.' Near the end, we are reminded of the persistence and intensity of his struggle as he prays in the Garden of Gethsemane: 'Father if you are willing remove this cup from me.' His words resonate to this day with those facing sad and difficult times in their own lives.

Christian living does not mean living without failure, nor does it mean being free from temptation. We are all personalities in the making, in the process of becoming, trying to cope with things that are often beyond us. Indeed one of the unnecessary burdens we carry is the notion that we must be perfect, for even in our best moments we can make bad choices and get things wrong. Oscar Wilde famously observed that he could resist everything but temptation, but perhaps another of his sayings is more apposite in this discussion: 'Every saint has a past and every sinner has a future.'

Some years ago a television play by Dennis Potter entitled *Son of Man* caused uproar. In it, Jesus was shown to be an eccentric who was unsure both of himself and his mission. In reaction, protesters insisted that the 'real' Jesus could not possibly be like that because he was the Son of God and must, therefore, be a cut above everyone else. But to claim that Jesus was some kind of superhuman being is to miss the whole point of the incarnation, a point made very clear in the letter to the Hebrews (4:15). 'For we do not have a high priest who is unable to sympathise with our weaknesses, but we have one who in every respect has been tempted as we are, yet without sin.' Jesus, like us, lived in the real world.

A prayer asks for 'grace to withstand the temptations of the world, the flesh and the devil'. It reminds us not only of personal weaknesses, but also of the fact that we live in a shoddy world where evil is ever-present and there is real pressure to give in. This is what happened to the followers of Jesus in those final days. Some of them were nakedly ambitious; others were suspicious and questioning; ultimately, all of them were terrified of the people in power. Thus, they abandoned Jesus one by one – but not he them. What saw them through was not their faithfulness but the refusal of Jesus to give up on them. Bishop F. R. Barry emphasises the God dimension in all this:

> Christianity, when it is true to its genius is able to believe
> in humanity recklessly, despite all that saddens and
> discourages, because it has seen the vision of God, the
> eternal source of all worth and wonder – lifting us up to
> become sons and daughters of God. In the long run those

men and women who have been most effective in changing and remodelling the present world, [are those] who have realised that goodness, in whatever form, is not in the end something that we produce, but something that claims us and is imparted to us by the eternal and unchanging goodness.

Perhaps the most important thing for all of us to be is honest with ourselves and about ourselves, recognising both our limitations and the distractions of the world around us that can so easily destroy our hopes for the future. Our ultimate and truest hope does not rest on anything we do, but on the generosity and love of God. One of the most reassuring features of our Lord's ministry, as recorded in the gospels, is that he always accepted people as they were, a point well made by the American theologian William Countryman when he wrote: 'The person you are now, the person you have been, the person you will be – this person God has chosen as beloved.'

Truly Human

It is important that Christians should not equate atheism with humanism. They are not one and the same.

Published 15 May 2010

It is interesting how words sometimes change to reflect the culture and the circumstances of the time. The word 'humanist', for example has, for many, come to represent non-believers, men and women of high principle who don't believe in God. However, that is by no means the whole story. There are many who would gladly identify themselves as Christian humanists and who see no difficulty in combining the two positions. Bishop Richard Harries maintains that the term 'humanist' was first used during the Renaissance by Christians who wished to assert the value of the human person. In the course of the debate, Pope Innocent III wrote a book entitled *On the Misery of Man*, which drew a response entitled *On the Excellency and Dignity of Man* by a certain Gianozzo Manetti. Harries argues that this was not anti-Christian as some might think, but rather an affirmation from within the Christian community of the value and dignity of man, who is made in the divine image.

The Feast of the Ascension is an event that has much to say about our common humanity. We miss a great deal by dwelling too much on the physical characteristics of the event; much more important is the thought that in our Lord's ascension our humanity also ascends. It might seem at first that to equate our humanity with that of Jesus is almost blasphemous. But while acknowledging our many imperfections, the plain fact is that ours is the humanity that he took and shared and transformed. In the course of his earthly life he experienced every possible human emotion and feeling – good days, bad days, acceptance and rejection, popularity and loathing, suffering and, ultimately, death. Christians believe that it was the same humanity that he took to the cross and, in the mystery we call the resurrection, lifted beyond death to a reality that is beyond words.

Herbert O'Driscoll, former Dean of Vancouver, writes about his days as an ordinand studying in Dublin and living at what was then known as the Church of Ireland Divinity Hostel in Mountjoy Square. He remembers in particular addresses given in the chapel by the great Archbishop Anthony Bloom, who sometimes stayed there when visiting the small Russian Orthodox community in Dublin. O'Driscoll recalls one such address:

> I realised that in many ways he was trying to enrich our images of the supreme moment we call the Ascension. Bloom was trying to get us to see that the event was not about our Lord's going away. Only when we realise this do we see that, far from being left comfortless, we are strengthened by the fact that our humanity has been exalted … a part of my humanity stands in the unimaginable light of the presence of God. I stand there, and each one of us stands there. Why and how? Because

Jesus stands there. When he ascended he took with him part of the humanity of each one of us. What more can we say?

There are of course those who find it difficult to hold such a belief and who would describe themselves as humanists. They are often people who have travelled some distance along the Christian path in terms of the values they live by but are unable to take that final step of faith – a position we must respect. There is no reason why we cannot join with them in celebrating the values we share and trying to promote them.

Christian faith, however, takes us much further in that valuing the person is not just a matter of personal opinion or collective agreement. It is a value that is given not invented or voted in. The gospel insists that people are of inestimable value because they are the children of God. And they are not just people in general, but individual women, men and children, each with a name, each having a priceless worth.

Let no one say we are worthless. God is not a foolish speculator; he would never invest in a worthless property.
(Erwin W. Lutzer)

A World Of Our Own

It is easy to point a finger at others, but three remain pointed at ourselves.

Published 27 October 2007

It is disturbing to look back through the centuries and reflect on actions and attitudes within the Church that were clearly inconsistent with basic Christian principles. Even allowing for the cultural and political influences of the times, it is difficult to justify the awful things done in the name of Christ that were blatant contradictions of everything he stood for. How, for example, could anyone justify the burning of so-called witches, the barbarism of the Inquisition, exploitation through slavery, the persecution of Jews or the hatred of gay people? But they did these things and believed they were right in what they did. That kind of thinking remains with us.

Pride is considered the worst of the seven deadly sins. It is an attitude which causes us to set ourselves at the centre of things; so that we become the measure of truth, of good and evil. It means celebrating one's own achievements or abilities to the detriment of others. It insists that 'we are better than the rest' and operates on both personal and communal levels. It is sobering to reflect on what that feeling of superiority led to in Germany under the Nazis, in South Africa during the apartheid era and more recently in attitudes towards immigrants on our own streets.

In his 2002 Nobel speech in Oslo, President Jimmy Carter said he believed that times were 'challenging and disturbing for those whose lives are shaped by a religious faith based on kindness towards each other'. Asked later to explain, he expressed his concern at the trend towards fundamentalism in all religions and where it can lead. He explained its rationale, saying: 'Increasingly, true believers are inclined to begin a process of deciding: "Since I am aligned with God, I am superior and my beliefs should prevail, and anyone who disagrees with me is inherently wrong," and the next step is "inherently inferior." The ultimate step is "subhuman," and then their lives are not significant.'

In St Luke's Gospel (18:11 ff) Jesus tells a parable about a man who went into the Temple to pray. He thanked God loudly that he wasn't 'like other people, thieves, rogues, adulterers'. He lists his religious virtues, which include fasting and giving generously to charity. He makes a particular point of belittling someone close by, 'this tax collector', who is only too aware of his shortcomings. That pointing finger epitomises an arrogance and a pride which encourages people 'to think more highly of themselves than they ought to think', often with deadly consequences.

That notion of being 'better than the rest' is not unknown within the Church. It is heard in inter-church exchanges, where too much time is spent pointing out the inadequacies of other traditions while overlooking the deficiencies in one's own. Little thought or concern is shown for the hurt caused or the damage done. A similar air of superiority is sometimes evident in the Church's engagement with the secular world. There is a tendency to devalue the goodness of people who have no formal religious commitment, people whose lives are rich in Christian virtue but who may find it difficult to sign up to traditional Church teachings. However, it is clear from the gospels that Jesus had no difficulty relating to people of different backgrounds and beliefs. Indeed one of the characteristics of his ministry was his acceptance of – and respect for – almost everyone he met. Condemnation was reserved for religious hypocrisy, as brilliantly illustrated in that Temple incident.

The late Archbishop Anthony Bloom of the Russian Orthodox Church suggested that humility was the appropriate antidote to pride: 'Basically humility is the attitude of one who stands constantly under the judgement of God. *Humility* comes from the Latin word *humus,* fertile ground. The fertile ground is there unnoticed, taken for granted, always there to be trodden upon … The more lowly, the more fruitful, because it becomes really fruitful when it accepts all the refuse of the earth … it has accepted the last place and cannot go any lower.' The Archbishop is reminding us that we belong to a serving and a caring church. History teaches that when we forget this fact, we, like previous generations, will get things badly wrong.

It was pride that changed angels into devils; it is humility that makes men as angels.

(St Augustine)

127

Things That Last

Pope Benedict consecrates the new cathedral Sagrada Familia in Barcelona.

Published 13 November 2010

Inscribed on the tomb of Sir Christopher Wren in St Paul's Cathedral, London are the words *Lector, Si monumentum requiris circumspice: [Reader, If you seek his memorial, look around you]*, an acknowledgement of the fact that he was the architect of that fine landmark building, set apart for the worship of God when it was consecrated in 1708. And just a week ago Pope Benedict was in Barcelona to consecrate another fine building, the Sagrada Familia Church, which was begun more than a hundred years ago and has yet to be completed.

There is something special about these great cathedrals and churches. They are links with the past, representing continuity and, perhaps in some minds, even permanence. It has always been like that and in St Matthew's Gospel (24:1–14) we read that people living in our Lord's time valued wonderful religious buildings too: 'some were speaking about the temple, how it was adorned with beautiful stones and gifts dedicated to God.'

One can only imagine then how shocked and angry they must have been when Jesus told them 'the days will come when not one stone will be left upon another; all will be thrown down'. He went on to talk of uncertain times ahead, of wars and earthquakes; plagues and persecution and much else – things that we would dread and rather not contemplate.

Conversely, the American theologian, Reinhold Niebuhr, saw possibilities in adversity. He observed that some of the most profound religious developments have come in times of national and international crisis. He pointed out that throughout the Old Testament, the prophets came to the fore at times when Israel was on the verge of collapse; that Christianity took root when Graeco-Roman culture was in decline, that St Augustine redefined Christianity as the Roman Empire was collapsing; and that the Protestant Reformation took place at a time of great unrest in Europe. It seems that in much the same way today, the Church is being renewed and reshaped by events outside its control and it is not a comfortable experience for everyone.

But the gospel encourages us not to lose our nerve in times of difficulty, for the Christian religion holds that our existence never ceases to have meaning even when chaos appears to reign. Our faith is centred, not on any human institution or structure or achievement, but on the will and purposes of God. These will prevail, despite our human frailty, which so often appears to frustrate them.

Niebuhr, who was writing in the mid-twentieth century offered this analysis, which has particular relevance for the Church today:

> So great is the power of human pride that even within the terms of the Christian faith man places his essential trust not in the ultimate character of God but in some achievement of the human spirit. The temptation to do

this is particularly great when these achievements are specially imposing; when the edifices of human genius have achieved a stability which seems to suggest their indestructibility. Hence periods of prosperity inevitably lead to a corruption of the Christian faith while periods of adversity prompt men to probe more deeply into the nature and meaning of life.

It is one thing to look around St Paul's Cathedral or the Sagrada Familia Church and marvel at the work of great men. However, it is even more important to see beyond their achievements the eternal God who gives all things meaning. A Church report reminds us: 'That in which we put our trust is essentially the constancy and reliability of God. His faithfulness consists in his unbreakable commitment to his people and, as the scriptures indicate, to his whole creation. He will never turn back from the love which binds him to the world and which remains his way with the world to the end of time. It is a way that embraces the "changes and chances" in all their arbitrary freedom, with the "eternal changelessness" of a love that bears, believes, hopes and endures all things.'

꿈

Holding On

A man of faith faces terminal cancer.

Published 2 October 2010

There are times in life when it can be difficult to hold on to one's faith, especially in times of personal anxiety or loss. People of no faith probably have no such problem, for they live in a world of chance and fate, where there are no questions to be asked and no answers expected. But for someone who believes in a God who is love the situation is entirely different. When life is hard, believers well understand the desperate cry of the psalmist: 'My God, my God, why, why, why...?'

In 1983, a well-known Church of England priest, Canon David Watson, conducted an ecumenical mission in St Paul's Church, Glenageary, Co. Dublin. He was based in a city church in York called St Michael le Belfry, but had an international reputation as a leading figure in the Church renewal movement of that time. On that Dublin visit Watson was a very sick man – he had been diagnosed with cancer a little while earlier – yet somehow he managed to inspire and encourage many who heard him speak about his own faith and the importance of it in difficult times.

In his book *Fear No Evil* he wrote: 'Eleven months have passed since the cancer in my body was first detected – eleven months of the limited life I am expected to have left. The future is bleak and I am getting used to people looking at me as a dying man under sentence of death. But nothing is certain; everything is a matter of faith.' He argued that the opposite of faith is fear and that 'fear is faith in what you do not want to happen'. He goes on to explain how he makes sense of his own faith in the terrible situation he was facing. 'God never promises to protect us from our problems, only to help us in them. If we leave God out of the picture, those difficulties might so strip away our sense of security that we feel vulnerable and afraid. On the other hand those same difficulties could drive us back to God and so strengthen our faith. We might feel just as vulnerable but we have to trust God because there is really no alternative; and then we discover God is with us in the dark as in the light, in pain as in joy.' David Watson died just a few months after that Dublin visit. He was fifty years old.

The disciples ask Jesus to increase their faith, a reminder that there is no such thing as an inner circle of believers who never ask questions and who never struggle to make sense of what is going on in their lives. One theologian has raised an interesting question about Jesus and his own suffering on the cross when he cried out that God had forsaken him. Had Jesus so totally embraced our human nature that just for a moment he lost faith feeling utterly alone and abandoned? That thought ought to allow us to feel a little more comfortable about our moments of uncertainty and doubt. At such times, however, we can also be strengthened by the faith of David Watson and others.

Archbishop Oscar Romero, whose own faith was tested to the limit (he was eventually murdered by his political enemies), had this to say about the cry of Jesus from the cross, 'My God, my God, why have you forsaken me?': '[Jesus] is not forsaken, but he feels the pain and anguish that our hearts must sometimes suffer. It is the psychology of suffering, to feel alone, to feel that no one understands. God is not failing us when we don't feel his presence. God is closer to you when you think he is farther away and doesn't hear you … It is then that prayer and religion have most merit; when one is faithful in spite of not feeling the Lord's presence.'

Getting It Wrong

As human beings, we sometimes love to hate. Thoughts on the threat of an American preacher to burn the Koran.

Published 18 September 2010

'We came to have a peaceful conversation with the pastor, to hear his grievance, to ask him to follow his own scripture about his enemies. His scripture teaches him to love his enemies.' This is the comment of a Florida-based Imam who had met the evangelical preacher Terry Jones, whose recent threat to burn copies of the Koran has caused uproar across America and beyond.

Jim Wallis, one American religious commentator observed: 'What Jones doesn't seem to understand is that the message he is really sending is a sacrilegious slap in the face of Jesus Christ. If Jones and his followers go through with their plans to burn the Koran, they might as well burn some Bibles too, because they are already destroying the teachings of Jesus. Jesus called his followers to be peacemakers, and to love not only their neighbours, but also their enemies; instead Jones and his church have decided to become agents of conflict and division.'

This controversy underlines the difficulty we have when dealing with fear and anger. A feature of the current controversy is the demonising of the Muslim community, which can be traced to the 9/11 outrages at the World Trade Centre in New York and elsewhere. Americans were deeply hurt by those events, and the families of the victims are still devastated.

But it does not belittle anybody's hurt to suggest, as the gospel does, that we must not allow ourselves to be imprisoned by an anger which is self-destroying. The future lies in our determination to work for a new world where peace and reconciliation are the order of the day.

Demonising those who are different to us in race, religion or culture is dangerous – and it is not confined to those we consider to be extremists. It can be found in the words and actions of people who consider themselves decent and respectable, yet who have a problem coping with difference. This was highlighted in the recent BBC programme *Who Do You Think You Are?* when the subject, actress Dervla Kirwan, discovered that in 1902 her great-great-grandfather Henry Kahn, a Dublin Jew, was sent to prison by Judge Frederick Falkiner for breaking windows. The judge refused to let him speak during his trial, misdirected the jury and told him: 'You are a specimen of your race and nation that cause you to be hunted out of every country.' There was uproar over these comments and, although the sentence was commuted, Henry Kahn, having lost his business, ended up with his family in the workhouse and died a broken man. It was a short step in thinking from that Dublin court in 1902 to the Holocaust a generation later.

Another 'specimen of [that] race and nation' points us in a completely different direction. Jesus refused to write people off. Several times he commended the Samaritans, who were hated by the Jews; he came to the aid of a centurion, an officer of the hated Roman occupying army; he accepted hospitality from a woman of ill repute. Throughout the gospel story, there is a pattern of accepting and tolerating difference; of seeing what is good in the individual, irrespective of who they were or where they came from. Space is found for those who hitherto had been excluded.

The attitude of Terry Jones and the 9/11 bombers will be used to argue that religion is an instrument of hatred and division. However, just as the proclaimed faith of 9/11 bombers bears no resemblance to the faith of many Muslims, the actions of Jones and his followers bear no resemblance to the faith of Christians. Prejudice and hatred are features of the human condition of which we are all capable, religious and non-religious alike. Religion at its best seeks to raise us to a new level of understanding what it means to be a citizen of the world.

Hatred and bitterness can never cure the disease of fear; only love can do that. Hatred paralyses life; love releases it. Hatred confuses life; love harmonises it. Hatred darkens life; love illumines it.

(Martin Luther King)

❦

Beyond Words

In 2012 the Spence family from Hillsborough, Co. Down lost three of its
members in a farming accident. How can anyone cope with such a loss?

Published 20 October 2012

It is deeply moving to hear people of faith saying how important
that faith is to them at times of personal loss. This was the case with
the Spence family from Hillsborough, Co. Down as they faced up to
the tragic loss of a father and his two sons in a farming accident.
Emma Spence spoke about her father and her brothers at the funeral
service in their local Baptist Church, and people were moved by her
composure and grace. She ended her address with these words:
'They were gentlemen, they were hard-working men, they were not
perfect but they were genuine, they were best friends. They were
godly men; they did not talk about God, they just did God. They
were just ordinary, God made them extraordinary.'

A few weeks later in Manchester two young policewomen were
killed when they answered what they believed to be a call for help

but which turned out to be something quite evil. Their chief constable Sir Peter Fahy, a Roman Catholic, spoke of the pain that he and his colleagues felt. He spoke about his faith, saying how important prayer is, especially at times like this when one feels helpless. He said that 'praying for the dead officers and their families was an expression of hope for them at a time of great need'.

In St Matthew's Gospel (20:20–8) the disciples James and John made a request to Jesus: 'Grant us to sit, one at your right hand and one at your left, in your glory.' They are firmly told that this was not in his gift. There is always the temptation in matters religious to think more highly of oneself or one's denomination in terms of closeness to Jesus, and therefore the truth. Some words from St John come to mind when we consider how Emma Spence and Peter Fahy, speaking out of different faith traditions, bore such authentic witness to the reality of God in their lives in times of distress. 'The wind blows wherever it pleases. You hear its sound, but you cannot tell where it comes from or where it is going. So it is with everyone born of the Spirit' (John 3:8).

Jesus talks about his passion and death, telling his followers that they too will face pain and suffering. 'The cup that I drink you will drink; and with the baptism with which I am baptised, you will be baptised' (Mark 10:39). The Christian faith has never claimed that we will escape the hard knocks that life brings. However, we have the assurance of strength given according to need, and the conviction that no matter how dark things may seem, 'joy cometh in the morning'.

That hope is explored further in these words from the riches of yet another great Christian tradition. In *The Diary of a Russian Priest*, Alexander Elchaninov wrote:

> Neither our natural attachment to life nor our courage
> in bearing suffering; neither earthly wisdom or even
> faith – however great – none of these can preserve us

from sorrow for the dead. Death is a twofold phenomenon: there is the death of the departed, and the
suffering and deadening in our own soul, occasioned by
painful separation. [The Christian] must not recoil when
faced with suffering nor remain impotently passive
before it. He must exert his spiritual powers to the
utmost in order to pass through suffering, and emerge
from it stronger, deeper, wiser.

No matter if we are weak in our faith and unstable in our
spiritual life – the love we bear towards the departed is
not weak; and our sorrow is so deep, precisely because
our love is so strong. Through the tension of our love,
we too shall cross the fatal threshold which they have
crossed. By an effort of our imagination, let us enter into
the world which they have entered; let us give more
place in our life to that which has now become their life;
and slowly, imperceptibly, our sorrow will be turned into
joy which no one can take from us.

Plain Truth

A cardinal tells us what he really thinks – after he died.

Published 6 October 2012

Cardinal Carlo Maria Martini died in Varese, northern Italy, on 31 August 2012, at the age of eighty-five. Two weeks earlier, he had given a remarkable interview, a 'spiritual testament', to be published after his death.

His strong faith and loyalty to the Church is evident from a long and distinguished ministry – yet in this interview he expresses deep concerns about the future. What is especially significant is that much of what he had to say about his own church could be said about many churches. Here is something of what he said:

> The church is tired. Our culture has become old, our churches and our religious houses are big and empty, the bureaucratic apparatus of the church grows, our rites and our dress are pompous. Do these things, however,

express what we are today? We find ourselves like the rich young man who went away sad when Jesus called him to be his disciple. I know that we can't let everything go easily. At least, however, we can seek people who are free and closest to their neighbour, like Archbishop Romero and the Jesuit martyrs of El Salvador. Where are the heroes among us who can inspire us? By no means do we have to limit them by the boundaries of the institution.

Martini suggested three instruments of renewal, the first of which was conversion. He argued that the Church must recognise its errors and follow a radical path of change beginning at the top: 'Questions about sexuality, and all the themes involving the body, are an example. We have to ask ourselves if people still listen to the advice of the church on sexual matters. Is the church still an authoritative reference in this field, or simply a caricature in the media?' This is significant given recent comments by former President McAleese about the high suicide rate among young gay men. She said many are driven into a place that is 'dark and bleak', and questioned the influence of Church teaching in these matters.

The second instrument the cardinal suggests is the scriptures:

Only those who perceive this Word in their heart can be part of those who will help achieve renewal of the church, and who will know how to respond to personal questions with the right choice. Neither the clergy nor ecclesiastical law can substitute for the inner life of the human person. All the external rules, the laws, the dogmas, are there to clarify this internal voice and for the discernment of spirits.

Thirdly he emphasised the importance of the sacraments:

> The sacraments are not an instrument of discipline, but a help for people in their journey and in the weaknesses of their life. Are we carrying the sacraments to the people who need new strength? I think of all the divorced and remarried couples, to extended families. They need special protection. A woman, for instance, is abandoned by her husband and finds a new companion, who takes care of her and her three children. This second love succeeds. If this family is discriminated against, not only is the mother cut out [from the church] but her children are also. If the parents feel like they're outside the church, and don't feel its support, the church will lose the future generation.

The cardinal concluded:

> The church is 200 years behind the times. Why doesn't it stir? Are we afraid? I'm old and sick, and I depend on the help of others. Good people around me make me feel their love. This love is stronger than the sentiment of distrust that I feel every now and then with regard to the church in Europe. Only love defeats exhaustion. God is love.

There will be many, clergy and lay, who will identify with these sentiments. These are the words of a pastor who, like Jesus, cares about people. They are also the words of a prophet directed at churches that are preoccupied with things that don't really matter. Is it not just possible that the Holy Spirit is the source of these challenging words and we are too tired or too busy to listen?

The Outsider

A tribute to Mary Raftery, who courageously spoke up for the victims of abuse.

Published 28 January 2012

Archbishop Diarmuid Martin was kind and gracious in the comments he made about the journalist Mary Raftery at the time of her death:

> I believe the truth makes us free; bringing the truth out is always a positive thing, even though it may be a painful truth. I believe that through her exposition of the sins of the past and of the moment the church is a better place – a better place for children and a place which has learned many lessons.

Some were less fulsome in their tributes, complaining that in focussing on the abuse issue she failed to acknowledge what was good in the Church. However, they don't see what the Archbishop has seen: that no matter how much good the Church does in other respects, nothing could excuse the evils exposed by Mary Raftery, often in the face of resistance. The damage done to the Christian cause was not done by the exposure of the evil, but by the evil itself.

It is difficult to accept criticism of something that we are part of, especially when it comes from outside. But we need to pay attention to what others say and think about us. God sometimes uses outsiders to point us back to what matters.

This happened in a spectacular way in Old Testament times when the Jewish people were in exile. They believed that as the chosen people of God that they could come to no harm and ignored warnings to the contrary. As a result, their country was overrun and they ended up in Babylon. Their distress is captured in the words of psalm 137, words which were popularised by the music group Boney M in their 1978 hit: 'By the rivers of Babylon, there we sat down, yea we wept, when we remembered Zion/For there they that carried us away captive required of us a song/How shall we sing the Lord's song in a strange land?'

The Jews were freed when the Persian king Cyrus defeated the Babylonians in 539 BC. He allowed them to return home and to rebuild Jerusalem and its Temple. Cyrus, to the Jews a heathen king, an outsider, is described as God's anointed, a chosen instrument to restore a chosen people who had lost their way. Thanks to that outsider they would again 'sing the Lord's song', and in their own land.

David Jenkins, former bishop of Durham, held a candid view of the Church: 'It is simply not true that there is anywhere a church guaranteed to get it right under God. To claim this or to behave as if this were so is to present an implausible and unworthy picture of God. For if it were the case that there exists a church which is bound to be right when it speaks for God, speaks of God, or acts for God, then we should all be bound to be atheists. For the records of all the churches contain acts of inhumanity, declarations of stupidity and indications of triumphalism, arrogance and insensitivity which are a disgrace to God – or indeed to ordinary humanity.'

The churches must recognise the importance of what others say and think, for their mission is not to themselves, but to the wider world. A central part of that mission is the promotion of healing and reconciliation at every level of society; yet too often we are seen as a source of division and rivalry. As yet another octave of prayer for Christian unity ends, it is difficult to find many signs of a real desire at a leadership level to respond to the prayer of Jesus: 'That they may be one.' We seem unwilling or unable to acknowledge that the Church's brokenness is a scandal, a grave sin; the contradiction of what she exists to be and a serious obstacle to her task. It is much, much easier to blame others for the decline of religious influence: the secularists, the humanists and all the other 'ists' who dare to ask questions when we do not practice what we preach.

That's what Mary Raftery did – and she, the outsider, was right.

Freedom to Choose

In praise of Maeve Binchy and Katie Taylor.

Published 25 August 2012

Some years ago the journalist Richard Ingrams edited an anthology entitled *Jesus: Authors Take Sides*. In it he assembled the views of well-known authors about Jesus and his significance ranging from those who held traditional Christian views to those who rejected them. For some, it wasn't the person of Jesus that was the problem but those who claimed to represent him – and who so often misrepresented him.

Maeve Binchy, who sadly died recently, left a wonderful legacy, not only of literary achievement, but also as a fine human being. She made it possible to say 'I have lost my faith', despite the fact that she had been brought up in a devout and loving Christian home. This took courage in an Ireland where religion was the done thing; it was expected of everyone, and those who questioned it were considered suspect.

The blind expectation, however, that everyone must believe – and believe in a particular way – failed to recognise that coercion and faith are incompatible. Faith, by its very nature, is born of the freedom to choose, and the suppression of that freedom meant that important faith questions were left unanswered. Conformity was the order of the day, with many sharing the English schoolboy's view of religion: 'believing wot you know ain't true.'

Theo Dorgan, writing in *The Irish Times*, said this about religion:

> I found that I was an agnostic, not an atheist. Even as a gawky and often simple-minded teenager I thought it extraordinarily presumptuous to claim that there could be no God because I did not believe in one. I mean I allowed for the possibility that I might be proved wrong. I am still unpersuaded by the many ingenious 'proofs' for the existence of God that thinkers down through the ages have offered, and I am equally unpersuaded by the hectoring tone and hysterical righteousness of 'scientific' campaigning atheists.

Archbishop Dermot Martin spoke recently of the need to present the message of Jesus Christ in a manner that responds to the challenges adults face regarding their faith in today's world: 'Being a Christian today can never involve shallow flight from the realities and complexities of the modern world.' He suggested that the emphasis on religious education in schools, although important, has perhaps taken away attention from the need for an adult religious education one which 'treats men and women as adults' and addresses 'the questions which adult Christians have to face as they live their faith in today's changing world'.

In St John's Gospel (6:66–71) we read of an encounter between Jesus and Peter. Jesus had claimed that he alone was the source of strength and sustenance for his followers. We are told that upon hearing this, 'many of his disciples … no longer went about with him.' He does not damn them to hell, instead he makes it clear that people must choose by asking those still with him 'Do you also wish to go away?' Peter responds: 'Lord to whom can we go? You have the words of eternal life. We have come to believe and know that you are the Holy One of God.'

Peter and those who remained with him must have wavered like the others, but they stayed because of the spiritual vitality and truthfulness of the message of the one they had come to know as the Son of God. And what is significant is that despite setbacks and denials along the way, they stayed until the end, sometimes at great cost. A path that has been chosen by millions ever since.

In Richard Ingram's book, Philip Toynbee, one of the contributors, said this about Jesus: 'Jesus of Nazareth: that scarcely visible young man; but from whom light streams forward into the New Testament, into the early Church, into all later history.'

God will never be without witnesses, who turn up in all sorts of unexpected places – even in a boxing ring. When Katie Taylor won her Olympic gold medal millions applauded her success but at every opportunity she declared her faith in Jesus Christ and in one interview asked 'where would I be without God in my life?' That's really what Peter says, along with people of faith everywhere.

In Tune With The Gospel

'I'd like to teach the world to sing in perfect harmony.' The West-Eastern Divan Orchestra at the London Proms.

Published 11 August 2012

Last month a remarkable group of young musicians were in London to give several performances, including Beethoven's symphonies, as part of this year's promenade season.

The West-Eastern Divan youth orchestra is a youth orchestra based in Seville, Spain, consisting of musicians from countries in the Middle East and from Egyptian, Iranian, Israeli, Jordanian, Lebanese, Palestinian, Syrian and Spanish backgrounds. The Argentine-Israeli conductor Daniel Barenboim and the late Palestinian-American academic Edward Said founded the orchestra in 1999 with the intention of promoting understanding between Israelis and Palestinians and paving the way for a peaceful and fair solution to the Arab-Israeli conflict. Barenboim explains: 'The Divan is not a love

story, and it is not a peace story. It has very flatteringly been described as a project for peace. It isn't. It's not going to bring peace,
whether you play well or not so well. The Divan was conceived as a
project against ignorance: a project against the fact that it is absolutely essential for people to get to know each other, to understand what
the other thinks and feels, without necessarily agreeing with it.'

The London performances included Beethoven's Ninth Symphony. This symphony is best known perhaps for the great 'Ode to
Joy', which is a celebration of the brotherhood and unity of all
mankind; thus, it echoes the hopes and ambitions of the founders of
the orchestra. The Ode urges humankind to come together to enjoy
the wonder and beauty of the world. We are encouraged to live as
human beings, aware of the divine reality that stands over all human
efforts.

The existence of this orchestra and the music it plays represent a
dream, a hope, an instinct that lurks in all of us for a just and
peaceful world. We are appalled by the terrible suffering being
inflicted on so many innocent people in Syria and other places of
conflict, and feel helpless. An Old Testament reading (2 Samuel 18)
conveys the awfulness of human loss and grief – often a consequence
of human madness – as a father, in this case King David, laments the
death of his son in battle: 'O my son Absalom, my son, my son
Absalom! Would that I had died instead of you, O Absalom, my son,
my son!'

One of the Divan musicians described the orchestra 'as a human
laboratory that can express to the whole world how to cope with the
other' which is what the Christian Church is supposed to be about
but so often fails. In the letter to the Ephesians (4:26 ff) we read:

> Be angry but do not sin; do not let the sun go down on
> your anger, and do not make room for the devil. Let no
> evil talk come out of your mouths, but only what is
> useful for building up, as there is need, so that your

words may give grace to those who hear. And do not grieve the Holy Spirit of God, with which you were marked with a seal for the day of redemption. Put away from you all bitterness and wrath and anger and wrangling and slander, together with all malice, and be kind to one another, tender-hearted, forgiving one another, as God in Christ has forgiven you.

Daniel Barenboim is a realist in that he knows that no one person, however brilliant or well intentioned, can bring peace and healing to a troubled and divided world. What he does know, however, is that one can make a difference within one's own sphere of influence and that presents all of us with a challenge.

As Christians we need have no illusions about the difficulties facing anyone seeking to promote reconciliation and peace at any level. It is a task that has no defined limits because all of life belongs to God and all brokenness needs his healing touch. But it is a divine mission in which, through baptism, we are called to play our part. If the task seems too momentous, a good place to begin is with oneself and one's personal relationships; there is often something there needing attention.

Nearer My God To Thee

The centenary of the sinking of the Titanic.

Published 7 April 2012

It is difficult to explain why the loss of the Titanic a century ago still fascinates people across the world. I recall some years ago attending a crowded lecture in Tallahassee University in the United States when Dr Robert Ballard gave an account of his role in the discovery of the lost ship. Writing in *The Irish Times*, Donald Clarke questioned the appropriateness of some of the planned commemorative events suggesting that a little more restraint might be in order. He was right; however we look at it, this was a terrible tragedy for everyone involved.

One hundred years ago next Wednesday the great liner raised anchor off Queenstown (Cobh) and set sail for New York. Imagine the thrill and the excitement of the people on board, some 2300 passengers and crew. Imagine their hopes for the future as they set out for the New World on the grandest ship afloat. In a farewell letter sent from Cobh, one young man wrote: 'We are having glorious weather and the sun is shining most magnificently. Well dear mother I hope everyone at home is in good health and that things are quite alright. Give my love to all at home and tell them I shall write more letters when I get to the other side. I must now close with fondest love from your loving son. Will.'

Within hours those hopes and dreams had become a nightmare and worse. When it was all over, some 1500 men, women and children had lost their lives and countless others – survivors and bereaved family members – were left grief stricken.

Several aspects of this tragedy speak directly to us today. Firstly, it is a reminder of our vulnerability and our mortality. It teaches us that despite all the achievements of science and technology – and they are many – we can never have total control of our destiny; we are always travelling into the unknown.

It is said that as the ship foundered the musicians played the hymn tune 'Nearer My God To Thee'. This raises the question: where was God in all the anguish and despair? The Christian response is not found in some neat theory or speculation, but in the events of Holy Week and Easter where Jesus experienced every conceivable form of suffering: physical, emotional and spiritual. His desperate cry of 'why, why' suggested that he even felt abandoned by God, something any of us can feel in times of pain and sorrow.

But the story does not end in the despair of Good Friday or the ghostly silence of the day following. Easter changes everything; it tells us that God does not abandon us, that he is present and active into the beyond even when the world seems empty of his presence. Holy Week and Easter combine to tell us that lives that have been touched by God are indestructible, as St Paul put it, 'nothing in all creation [not even death] will be able to separate us from the love of God in Christ Jesus our Lord.'

We may find this difficult to believe because it is too much to hope for, but we are in good company, for that is exactly what the disciples felt on that first Easter morning. Initially they thought the body of Jesus had been stolen. When reports began to emerge that Jesus had been seen some went into hiding, and others refused point blank to believe it. But as the evidence increased and the possibility became certainty, the once scattered and frightened followers of Jesus emerged to tell the world of their extraordinary experience. So, it is perfectly in order to wonder, to ask questions because it is part of the faith process which is described by Archbishop William Temple as 'transition from sight to faith; from outward companionship to inward communion'.

Bishop Desmond Tutu explains Easter thus: 'Easter means hope prevails over despair. Jesus reigns as Lord of Lords and King of Kings … Easter says to us that despite everything to the contrary, his will for us will prevail, love will prevail over hate, justice over injustice and oppression, peace over exploitation and bitterness.'

In Search Of Truth

The amazing Professor Stephen Hawking.

Published 14 January 2012

Last Sunday, 8 January 2012, the distinguished scientist Stephen Hawking celebrated his seventieth birthday. His achievements are truly amazing given the fact that he suffers from motor neurone disease, with which he was diagnosed when he was only twenty-one, and is almost completely paralysed. This is a man to be honoured and celebrated not only for his courage but also for his intellect: he makes us think.

Although usually represented as anti-religious, Hawking's position is more complicated than that. He claims not to be religious in the normal sense and believes that the universe is governed by the laws of science, but goes on to say that 'the laws may have been decreed by God, but God does not intervene to break the laws'. A similar point was made long ago by a psalmist who wrote: 'He [God] has given them a law which shall not be broken.'

Some people of faith feel threatened by people like Stephen Hawking, but we should value their searching and questioning. The ultimate aim for all of us has to be the discovery of truth; truth which has yet to be fully revealed and understood. St Paul, speaking from a religious standpoint, reminds us that 'we know in part and we prophesy in part'. The same has to be said of science; and when scientists comment on religious or spiritual matters they are simply stating opinions, not facts.

Elizabeth Basset, an English spiritual writer and conductor of retreats, spoke of life as a longing for meaning and a longing for God:

> Life is a search for this 'something', a search for something or someone to give meaning to our lives, to answer the question who am I, why am I here, what is the purpose of my life? I believe that this great need we all feel is caused by a longing which cannot be satisfied by the goals we set ourselves in this journey of life. There are countless ways in which the longing can be expressed, by poets and painters, musicians and dancers, and by so many of those whose talent is for living and loving in awe and worship. Perhaps the whole of life is concerned with this yearning. Nothing can be left out, but it carries us into death and beyond when we dare to hope that we shall come face to face with the source of all our longing.

In Psalm 139 the writer explores our identity 'O Lord you have searched me out and known me; you know my sitting down and my rising up; you discern my thoughts from afar.' Whatever about our longing for God, this psalmist has no doubts about God's constant awareness and knowledge of us: 'If I take the wings of the morning and dwell in the utter most parts of the sea, even there your hand shall hold me. If I say "Surely the darkness will cover me and the light around me turn to night," even darkness is no darkness with you; the night is as clear as the day.' In this age of forensic science – and especially DNA, the proof of unique personal identity – it is fascinating to reflect on the words of this psalm, written over two thousand years ago. The author suggests that we are not just known to God in some general way, an anonymous speck of humanity, but that we are known personally and individually from the beginning of life and throughout: 'I thank you for I am fearfully and wonderfully made ... My frame was not hidden from you when I was made in secret and woven in the depths of the earth. Your eyes beheld my form, as yet unfinished; already in your book were all my members written.'

Long ago, St Augustine suggested that it is God himself who prompts our search for him, as well as and our need for meaning and self-understanding: 'You move us to delight in praising you; for you have formed us for yourself and our hearts are restless till they find rest in you.'

'A Little Child Shall Lead Them'

The Tipperary Peace award is presented to Malala Yousafzai, the amazing young woman from Pakistan who was shot by the Taliban.

Published 24 August 2013

Some, perhaps many, will identify with the very human difficulty recounted in the call of the prophet Jeremiah, who was less than enthusiastic when he was called by God to assume the role of prophet at a time of national crisis. His reaction was to make excuses: he was too young, he was only a boy. In the exchange that follows he is told: 'Do not say, "I am only a boy"; for you shall go to all to whom I send you, and you shall speak whatever I command you. Do not be afraid of them, for I am with you to deliver you, says the Lord' (Jeremiah 1:7).

Jeremiah probably genuinely felt he did not have the ability or the experience to take on such a grave responsibility. However, he was overlooking the God dimension, the miracle that God calls inadequate and sinful people to be instruments of his transforming work in the world. All that is asked of them is that they remain faithful and leave the rest to God.

That is easier said than done, especially when we consider the scale of the task due to the evil and suffering that seem to dominate our world. Yet it is important to distinguish between global areas of concern, where individually we have little authority, and more immediate spheres of influence such as family and local community, where we can make a difference. Each one of us right now can make this a better world for someone, somewhere by a simple act of kindness or generosity.

St Luke's Gospel (13:10 ff) reminds us that religion can get in God's way. Jesus is teaching in the Synagogue on the Sabbath when he sees a woman in the congregation who has been crippled for half a lifetime – and he heals her. The leader of the synagogue is indignant and condemns Jesus. For him the act of healing was work, and work, according to his understanding of the law, was not permitted.

In his book, *Living the Gospel Stories Today*, John Pritchard, the Bishop of Oxford, suggests that this event poses questions for the Church today.

> Have we taken the gospel that gives a crippled woman a straight back and made it into an intricate system of rules and rituals, of dogmas and doctrines? Have we made a story into a system, and in the process locked out the sun? We all have a Pharisee in us just waiting to pop out. We can all play a religious game with our faith, admiring the aesthetics of it but missing the blazing reality of it. Enjoying the shape and sound of it, except when it comes in the shape of a bent back becoming straight and the sound of a woman crying with joy.

Last Tuesday, a young woman from Pakistan received the Tipperary Peace award. Malala Yousafzai was shot last year by the Taliban in an effort to silence her campaign to promote the educational rights of girls and women. She was very seriously injured and was lucky to survive. In July she addressed the United Nations in New York:

> I speak – not for myself, but for all girls and boys. I raise up my voice – not so that I can shout, but so that those without a voice can be heard. Those who have fought for their rights: Their right to live in peace. Their right to be treated with dignity. Their right to equality of opportunity. Their right to be educated.
>
> Dear Friends, on the 9th of October 2012, the Taliban shot me on the left side of my forehead. They shot my friends too. They thought that the bullets would silence us. But they failed. And then, out of that silence came, thousands of voices. The terrorists thought that they would change our aims and stop our ambitions but nothing changed in my life except this: Weakness, fear and hopelessness died. Strength, power and courage was born.

God surprises us with the people he calls to be prophets – among them young people. Malala celebrated her sixteenth birthday a few weeks ago.

c> *(decorative ornament)*

Beyond The Pain

Facing a New Year by letting the past go – the Mandela Way.

Published 28 December 2013

As the year 2013 comes to a close, people will experience differing reactions. Those who have had a difficulty year will be glad to see the end of it, whereas for those on whom fortune has smiled it will be a different matter. However, all are united in the hope that, as we face the uncertainties of a new year, all will go well for us and those we care about.

In the numerous tributes paid to Nelson Mandela, many have commented on his humility, and his capacity to forgive those who treated him so badly. It is almost beyond belief that in twenty-seven years of harsh imprisonment he never gave up hope. Mandela believed in the future and encouraged others to do the same – a good example to all, not just at the beginning of a new year, but throughout it. When he was released, he refused to become a prisoner of the past; his belief in the future set him free. This is something most of us are not good at. We hold on to resentments against family members and others. We find it difficult to let go of those occasions where we feel we have been wronged or let down. Mandela teaches us that this is not a good place to be and that facing the future with confidence and optimism makes sense: both are important aspects of the Christian life.

Christianity had an important part to play in Mandela's life and the political cause he espoused. He was educated in a Methodist college and he grew up in a land where leading churchmen opposed apartheid. One of these was Bishop Trevor Huddleston, whose book *Naught For Your Comfort*, published in 1957, was a powerful repudiation of the evil of apartheid. It challenged those who supported the system – and especially those church leaders who justified or excused it. For Huddleston, living by Christian standards in the modern world would always be costly. A recent reviewer commented: 'This book is still astonishing ... What it has to say about apartheid is riveting, but what is more astonishing is the way it describes the way in which people can mistreat others and how they can justify what they are doing because it is, supposedly, for the best.' A warning for today's world.

Desmond Tutu, a protégé of Trevor Huddleston and one of Mandela's closest friends, speaks of the challenge facing society not only in South Africa, but everywhere: 'The Church of God has to be the salt and the light of the world. We are the hope of the hopeless, through the power of God. We must transfigure a situation of hate and suspicion, of brokenness and separation, of fear and bitterness. We have no option. We are the servants of the God who reigns and cares.' In other words, we can help create conditions in which it is possible to be hopeful.

The scriptures encourage us as individuals and as communities to look to the future with confidence. The Old Testament reading from Isaiah (63) speaks of God present among his people caring for them: 'It was no messenger or angel but his presence that saved them; In his love and in his pity he redeemed them; he lifted them up and carried them all the days of old.'

St Matthew's Gospel (2:13–23) points to the presence of God in the person of Jesus under threat from King Herod. Scholars may debate the historicity or other aspects of this event, but it is clear that Jesus lived in a dangerous world. He was born in circumstances not unlike Syrian babies born in refugee camps this very day. And we are reminded that as an adult Jesus knew what it was to suffer: 'Because he himself was tested by what he suffered, he is able to help those who are being tested.'

As Nelson Mandela was laid to rest these words were said: 'Beyond the absence there is hope; beyond the pain there is healing; beyond the brokenness there is wholeness; beyond the turmoil there is peace; beyond the hurting there is heaven; beyond the silence God speaks.'

Who Will Show Us Any Good?

The rape and murder of a young woman in India and the killing of a garda remind us of the evil that stalks our world.

Published 9 February 2013

The Bible used by President Obama for the oath-taking ceremony at his recent inaugural was once owned by Abraham Lincoln. Lincoln was noted for his fine words, including many references to the importance of Christian values in public life. In 1861, for example, at his own inaugural, and with his country facing civil war, he said: 'Intelligence, patriotism, Christianity, and a firm reliance on Him [God], who has never yet forsaken this favoured land, are still competent to adjust, in the best way, all our present difficulty.'

Nowadays some claim that there is no need for religion at all, and that the human race can, of itself, improve; they might even dismiss as superstition the faith of those who think otherwise. Alistair Campbell, who was Tony Blair's Director of Communications, famously remarked: 'We don't do God.' But when we consider the

164

awfulness around us – the callous murder of a Garda, the rape and murder of a young woman in India, not to mention wars in Syria and elsewhere – it is difficult to be optimistic about our capacity to change for the better. We are what we are: always frail, sometimes fallen. Christians believe that we cannot change by tinkering with our minds or forcing our feelings; that change for the good only takes place when we engage with the great mystery we call God.

It is difficult to talk about religious experience. We hesitate because we don't want to appear pious, or we are afraid that we won't be taken seriously. Yet people do have such experiences. Simone Weil was a French philosopher and social activist. Born in 1909 into a Jewish family, Weil witnessed the destruction of Europe first hand, especially the rise of fascism and the horrors that followed. She was deeply troubled by these developments and actively opposed them. While visiting a monastery she had a powerful religious experience in which she said that 'Christ himself came down and took possession' of her. Weil claimed that she grew up 'within the Christian inspiration', despite her Jewish background. Although she was committed to Christianity, Weil was not a member of any church. She refused baptism, arguing that her faith included and embodied the truths of non-Christian and even heretical traditions. She used Christ's incarnation to fortify this argument, claiming that in becoming human Christ took on the flesh of all people and all cultures. (Was she suggesting that our concept of church is too narrow?) It is difficult for us to explain or get behind her conversion experience; we can only interpret it by recognising what followed.

It is similarly difficult to explain adequately the Transfiguration of our Lord. When Jesus climbs that mountain, he is not preoccupied with self, but identifies himself with the God who is love. All of his actions flow from that awareness. We understand a great deal when we remember that this event anticipates the final journey of Jesus to

Jerusalem and his crucifixion. The journey up that mountain, far from being a moment of escape, is a moment of acceptance of what is to come. However – and this is key – it is an acceptance that is made possible by the certainty that God is in control of the outcome.

St Paul makes that point when he spells out the hope God gives to all of us in this world of too much suffering and loss: 'Who shall separate us from the love of Christ? Shall tribulation or distress, or persecution, or famine, or nakedness, or peril or sword? No, in all these things we are more than conquerors through him who loved us' (Roman 8:35). The theologian Karl Barth, himself influenced by the suffering caused by two world wars, makes a connection between transfiguration and the pain we feel today: 'Thus our tribulation, without ceasing to be tribulation, is transformed. We suffer as we suffered before, but our suffering is no longer a passive perplexity, but is transformed into a pain which is creative, fruitful, full of power and promise.'

cℐℴ

Last Man Standing

No one should ever say that faith is easy. Some of the greatest saints knew that better than most.

Published 1 June 2013

The term 'dark night of the soul' is sometimes used to describe a crisis in our relationship with God. It is associated with the writings of St John of the Cross, a Carmelite friar who lived in the sixteenth century and who knew how difficult it could be to stay the journey of faith. He was not alone in this. St Thérèse of Lisieux spoke of her struggle and is said to have told her fellow nuns, 'If you only knew what darkness I am plunged into.' More surprisingly perhaps, according to letters released in 2007, Mother Teresa of Calcutta is said to have had similar difficulties over some time.

It is important to know that it is not unusual to experience such feelings, however, it is equally important to treat them as opportunities in which we can seek a deeper knowledge of God and his will for us.

The Bible has many examples of women and men of faith questioning and searching. Elijah, that lively prophet of the 9th century BC, is a prime example. His record is a mixture of popular stories and significant intervention in high level political action. On the one hand he is the holy man of folklore, fed by birds, who miraculously provides food and oil for a poor widow. On the other hand he single-handedly confronts Jezebel's prophets and denounces the abuse of power.

Elijah knew what it was to become disillusioned. In desperation, he withdrew to the desert, overwhelmed by a sense of failure. He believed that he had been God's only hope and that his best efforts had been in vain. And not only was *he* a failure, but so were those who had gone before him: 'It is enough; now O Lord take away my life for I am no better than my fathers.' They had worked and witnessed and died in the service of God, but seemed to have achieved little. It is worth noting how this exchange ends: there in that lonely desert place, God touched him and provided for his renewal and spiritual rejuvenation. It wasn't up to him after all; God was still in control.

Some church people probably feel like that today as they consider falling church attendances and an ageing membership. Parents in particular are bound to feel sad when their children and grand-children opt out of church life. There are signs, however, that a religion of convention is giving way to a religion of conviction and commitment. This will happen wherever the Church is faithful to Jesus Christ rather than itself, and wherever people are *living* rather than *discussing* the faith.

Elijah has a special significance for those engaged in ministry. He reminds us that ministry can be lonely at times and indeed discouraging. His cry of 'I, even I only, am left' will strike a chord with many – especially older clergy, who have lived through so much change. Elijah had to be reminded that his work was only a small part of something greater and directed by God himself. To the despairing cry 'only I am left', God tells Elijah that he has another 'seven thousand in Israel' witnessing to his rule. We need to remember and celebrate the fact that across the world, wonderful things are being done today in the name of Jesus Christ, and that it is still possible to play a part, however small.

In her book *Ascent to Love*, Ruth Burrows suggests that what St John of the Cross describes as 'Dark Night' is not only a religious phenomenon: 'Bereavement, disappointment, failure, old age, these and countless other human experiences engulf us in the night. All of them confront us with our finitude, raise fundamental questions on human existence and contain a challenge to accept our human vocation. But every human being is for God and an openness for God. It is not only around us who know his name but around every single person that the sun is shining, seeking an entrance. God uses every occasion to illuminate us and his illumination is often perceived as darkness.'

Let's Move On

World leaders show the way to peace and reconciliation.

Published 9 March 2013

Some weeks ago, an interview with Aung San Suu Kyi, the Burmese leader, on the BBC radio programme *Desert Island Discs* gave listeners the opportunity to hear this extraordinary woman speak about her life's work. Her bravery and determination has inspired people everywhere – a fact worth noting at a time when politics has been discredited in too many places.

In his book *The Lady and the Peacock*, Peter Popham describes the sacrifices that Kyi made and the dangers that she faced standing up to a brutal military regime. She was separated from her husband and children, imprisoned and spent over fifteen years under house arrest. According to Popham: 'Her isolation deepened. She had no visitors. To maintain solidarity with her comrades in jail who would have starved without relatives and friends to provide food for them, she refused to accept food from the regime.'

In an interview Kyi explained how her health was affected: 'Sometimes I didn't have enough money to eat. I became so weak from malnourishment that my hair fell out and I couldn't get out of bed. Every time I moved my heart went thump thump thump and it was hard to breathe. Then my eyes started to go bad.'

This amazing woman had every reason to be bitter, resentful and determined to have revenge. Instead, she emerged on to the world stage as an advocate of forgiveness and non-violence, encouraging her followers to learn to compromise without regarding it as a humiliation.

Richard Holloway, former Bishop of Edinburgh, says that genuine, unconditional forgiveness is the rarest of human virtues, but that when it happens it transforms lives. He makes the point that when Nelson Mandela walked out of his prison and set up a process that amounted to forgiving the agents of apartheid, he changed history. Mandela could see that the permanent quest for vengeance was ultimately self-defeating, and that only by confronting the past was it possible to find a way of forging a better future.

Aung San Suu Kyi and Nelson Mandela highlight the beauty of forgiveness, as well as how practical and sensible it is. They also remind us that it is costly and demanding, that it cannot be enforced or demanded, but has to be freely given.

In St Luke's Gospel (15) we read the story of the prodigal son. It describes the gracious welcome home of a wayward and exploitative son and the negative reaction of the brother who had stayed at his father's side and served him well. It is a situation that will strike a chord in some households. On a human level, it illustrates the rivalries that can exist between siblings but it also highlights the overriding instinct of a parent not to abandon or disown his or her child.

The spiritual aspect of this story is hugely reassuring. It assures us that no matter how much we fail in life, or how far we fall, we are always within the reach of God's welcoming, forgiving love. We may find that difficult to understand because it is not how *we* behave; there are some we find it hard to forgive and we think that God should agree with us. St Paul's words, however, put us in our place: 'All have sinned and fall short of the glory of God.'

Adrian Hastings develops that notion when he points out that we are all part of a community of guilt. 'We need to recognise that it is an inevitable part of our moral being as humans that we are sinners, sharing every one of us in a quality of guiltiness. Perhaps we can only help people to cope with guilt if, first of all, we can agree on that. It is from within a community of the guilty that we have to approach guilt, not as people who stand outside or think that it is even possible to stand outside. There is no us and them.'

Fallen and Forgotten

Irishmen lost in World War I are at last remembered.

Published 2 November 2013

It's easy to forget that for many years the people of this island were unwilling – and in some cases forbidden – to enter each other's churches. This was a particular issue in Northern Ireland where such an action had political as well as religious significance. However, Unionist leader David Trimble did just that when he attended a funeral in a Roman Catholic Church. It was described as an occasion 'when politics gave way to decency'.

Politics gave way to decency in Dungarvan recently when a memorial was unveiled to the 1100 men and women from Waterford who died in the First World War. The idea had come about because many of them had no known graves and were not remembered anywhere. Among the names listed were those of three brothers killed in Flanders.

Because of political developments at home at that time, thousands of families across this island were unable to publicly express their grief because the political climate was so hostile. Irish soldiers of the First and Second World Wars could not be remembered with the respect and dignity they deserve, and grieving families were denied the support that communal sympathy provides at such times. It's a sad reminder of what can happen when politics and decency don't meet. It remains a difficulty for some on this island to this day.

A reading that is sometimes used at funerals begins: 'Death is nothing at all.' An understandable reaction would be that surely this cannot be true; death is terrible. It breaks our hearts and leaves us to grieve. They would take on a more helpful meaning, however, when we examine the source. They are part of a sermon on death preached by Canon Scott Holland in St Paul's Cathedral London in May 1910 in which he acknowledges the feelings we might have standing by the body of a loved one who has just died: the sense of grief and utter helplessness; a feeling that nothing can ever make this situation any better. But then, speaking out of his Easter faith, Scott Holland imagines what the person who has just died would want to say back by way of reassurance:

> Death is nothing at all. It does not count. I have only slipped away into the next room. Nothing has happened. Everything remains exactly as it was. I am I, and you are you, and the old life that we lived so fondly together is untouched, unchanged. Whatever we were to each other, that we are still. Call me by the old familiar name. Speak of me in the easy way which you always used. Put no difference into your tone. Wear no forced air of solemnity or sorrow. Laugh as we always laughed at the little jokes that we enjoyed together. Play, smile, think of me, pray for me. Let my name be ever the household word that it always was. Let it be spoken without an

effort, without the ghost of a shadow upon it. Life means all that it ever meant. It is the same as it ever was. There is absolute and unbroken continuity. What is this death but a negligible accident? Why should I be out of mind because I am out of sight? I am but waiting for you, for an interval, somewhere very near, just around the corner. All is well. Nothing is hurt; nothing is lost. One brief moment and all will be as it was before. How we shall laugh at the trouble of parting when we meet again!

This is All Souls' Day, a day when we commemorate the faithful departed; a day when many pause to remember those 'loved long since and lost awhile'. We do so as Christians, in the belief that 'neither death nor life, neither angels nor demons, neither the present nor the future, nor any powers, neither height nor depth, nor anything else in all creation, will be able to separate us from the love of God that is in Christ Jesus our Lord' (Romans 8:38–9). And politics has no say in the matter.

A Place Set Apart

We are richly endowed in this country with wonderful churches and cathedrals. But what makes them special?

Published 16 November 2013

A summer visit to St Laserian's Cathedral, Co. Carlow was a reminder of the rich heritage we have in our ancient cathedrals and churches. The Cathedral's website informs us that early in the seventh century St Gobban founded a monastery there and was succeeded by St Laserian. A Synod held there in 630 AD settled the date of Easter, which until then had been observed by the Celtic Church at a different time to Rome. The original building, probably wooden, was destroyed by fire and the present stone building was begun in the 12th century.

The history is wonderful – if only stones could talk. But in a way they do, for they speak not only of the past, but of the present faith community; they are a place set apart to remind us of things spiritual. This is especially true of churches, where succeeding generations have been baptised; nurtured in the faith; married and, at the end of their earthly lives, laid to rest in adjoining burial grounds. It has been said that since the stone was rolled away from the tomb of Jesus, stones have been moved ever since to create holy places that bear witness to the Easter hope.

Of course there is always a danger that church buildings can become a distraction, making us lose sight of what they are about. In St John's Gospel (2:19 ff) Jesus drops a bombshell when he forecasts the destruction of the great temple in Jerusalem. People had been commenting on its beauty, the stonework and gifts dedicated to God, when Jesus declares: 'As for these things that you see the days will come when not one stone will be left upon another; all will be thrown down' (Luke 21:6).

Imagine the shock, the disbelief of the people, not least his own disciples. Yet by the time St Luke's account of the gospel was available, the Temple was in ruins. Something greater had taken its place: the young Christian Church was sharing the Easter hope in a world where the things that people trusted in so often end in ruin.

In *A Journey Along the Oka*, Alexander Solzhenitsyn refers to the churches dotted across the Russian landscape: 'Travelling along country roads in central Russia you begin to understand why the Russian countryside has such a soothing effect. It is because of its churches. From far away they greet each other; from distant, unseen villages they rise toward the same sky. Wherever you may wander you are never alone; above the wall of trees, above the hayricks, even above the very curve of the earth itself, the dome of a belfry is always beckoning to you. But as soon as you enter a village, you realise that the churches which welcomed you from afar are no longer living.' This was common in the Communist era, when many churches were closed and barricaded.

T.S. Eliot also recognised what made a church special. In his poem 'Four Quartets', completed against the background of the

London Blitz, he explores man's relationship with time, the universe and God. He named the final section 'Little Gidding', after a small village in Huntingdonshire, where in 1625 the Rev. Nicholas Ferrar and his family formed a religious community, devoted to prayer. This town became a place of pilgrimage and retreat, and it is said that Charles I sought refuge there.

Eliot had visited the church in 1936; now in a world in turmoil, he finds in *Little Gidding* an answer to human despair and fallibility: 'You are not here to verify, instruct yourself ... You are here to kneel, where prayer has been valid.' In that last memorable line, we are told what makes a place holy and, therefore, special.

Faith That Delivers

The death of Father Alec Reid and the anniversary of the death of C. S. Lewis.

Published 30 November 2013

Father Alec Reid, who died last week, has been described as being the initiator of the peace process and the most tireless worker for it. We owe him much for his role in bringing some normality to the North. It is significant that it was 'a man sent from God' who helped point the way towards peace and away from entrenched political posturing and murderous violence. The Rev. Harold Good, former President of the Methodist Church and his partner in that work, spoke of them as stumbling pilgrims 'seeking to walk in the footsteps of Jesus, the same Jesus who called each of us ... into a ministry of reconciliation'.

Today, St Andrew's Day, we are reminded that God calls very ordinary people to do extraordinary things. When Andrew was convinced of the importance of Jesus, his response was to go and share his discovery with his brother Peter. The call of Peter the fisherman proved to be a hugely significant moment in the life of the Church.

God has always called women and men to point humankind beyond the superficiality of mere existence towards more profound insights into the meaning and purpose of life; but some, like C.S. Lewis, don't always respond with enthusiasm.

Last week, on the fiftieth anniversary of his death, a memorial was dedicated to Lewis's memory in London's Westminster Abbey. Described as one of the greatest writers and thinkers of his generation, Lewis is best known today for *The Chronicles of Narnia*, a series of fantasy novels which has been adapted for radio, stage, screen and television. What is often overlooked is that he is also considered to be one of the foremost Christian apologists of the twentieth century. He was born in Belfast in 1898 and baptised in the Church of Ireland parish of St Marks, Dundela. Although he would spend most of his adult life in England he was proud of his Irish heritage: 'There is no doubt the Irish are the only people: with all their faults, I would not gladly live or die with other folk.'

Lewis became an atheist as a teenager, an outlook reinforced by his experiences soldiering in the trenches of the First World War. Nevertheless, he struggled with questions of belief, once saying that 'a young atheist cannot guard his faith too carefully'.

His return to religious faith is described in his book *Surprised by Joy*. He first came to belief in God (Theism) but not the Christian understanding of God. He describes the struggle: 'You must picture me alone in that room night after night, feeling, whenever my mind lifted even for a second from my work, the steady, unrelenting approach of Him whom I so earnestly desired not to meet. That which I greatly feared had at last come upon me in the Trinity term of 1929. I gave in, and admitted that God was God, and knelt and prayed: perhaps, that night, the most dejected and reluctant convert in all England.' It would take more time before he would fully embrace the Christian faith and return to the Anglican tradition of his childhood. He said that he was brought into Christianity like a prodigal 'kicking, struggling, resentful and darting his eyes in every direction for a chance to escape'.

It is said that C.S. Lewis has in our time instructed more people in the reasonableness of the Christian faith than all the theological faculties in the world – mainly through the written word, much of it still in print. He is proof that intellectual integrity and faith in Jesus Christ are compatible, something the Christian Church needs to state more clearly and more often.

Soon, people will be put under pressure by what is called the Christmas rush. It is also the season of Advent, a time given to reflect on the hollow pride that allows us to think that we are self-sufficient, yet which buries real and deeper spiritual longings. As C.S. Lewis observed: 'A proud man is always looking down on things and people; and, of course, as long as you're looking down, you can't see something above you.'

The Beyond Dimension

Easter is our God-given hope.

Published 14 April 2007

Easter is about that 'beyond' dimension of life which is outside our control and understanding. Easter tells us that God has reached across the barrier of our greatest ignorance – our limited understanding of life and death – to reveal a hope which is beyond our understanding or our ability to give.

Sometimes people use the language of Easter when talking about new beginnings in their lives. For example, they might speak of new life when health is recovered after illness, or when a relationship is restored. An Easter meditation notes: 'We know death and resurrection in our closest loves. In marriage ... we know what it is to struggle on where there are no rewarding emotions. After there comes a point where the relationship flowers beyond our imagination and it is impossible to escape the knowledge that joy and happiness sprang out of the darkness and the pain.' There are renewal moments in most lives; however, the resurrection of Jesus Christ is not just a way of drawing attention to something we already know. The gospel which brought the Christian Church into being is proclaiming something which is new and beyond our experience. C.S. Lewis underlines this in his book *Miracles*: 'The Resurrection is the central theme in every Christian sermon reported in the Acts. The Resurrection, and its consequences were the "gospel" or good news which the Christian brought ... The first fact in the history of Christendom is a number of people who say they have seen the Resurrection.' This is placed in a wider setting in the Book of Revelation: 'I am the Alpha and the Omega, says the Lord' – an assertion that God stands before history, that he is the meaning of history and that it is in that context that we are to understand the historical event we call the resurrection.

Modern man often has difficulty here, for he is too quick to dismiss what he does not understand or cannot control. He places himself at the centre of things and behaves badly as a result. We see this in his attempt over centuries to manage and control the environment, a folly we are only beginning to acknowledge. This level of self-belief can deprive us of the capacity to wonder, and thereby limits our horizons spiritually, morally and in other ways. There is nothing new in this, in fact it is part of an age-old human dilemma. The author of the Book of Revelation lived under the rule of the Roman state, which was so sure of itself that it had decided that its emperors were gods. He belonged to a community that was being persecuted for challenging such self-belief. Imprisoned for his faith, he – like many before him and since – was sustained by the conviction that God was actively in control, and that Christ had overcome death and was present with him.

That sort of confidence did not come easily to the young Church. St John's Gospel (20) can, according to the English novelist Graham Greene, 'stand with the best eyewitness reports'. It reminds us of the disciples locked away in a room for fear of their lives. Thomas the doubter was with them, refusing point blank to accept second-hand accounts of the resurrection. This is a potent reminder that it is not always easy to believe; that it is alright at times to have doubts for faith after all implies doubt. Somehow those frightened and doubting men and women held on to the faith which said 'yes' to Jesus being alive again, and 'yes' to his being their Lord.

Do not abandon yourselves to despair. We are the Easter people and hallelujah is our song.

(Pope John Paul II)

Handling Things Unseen

The Russian Orthodox Church – more than a building.

Published 28 April 2007

Last Tuesday the body of Boris Yeltsin, former President of the Russian Federation, was brought to the Cathedral of Christ the Saviour in Moscow to lie in State before a requiem the following day. The event and the place tell us important things about the life of the Church and about a faith that is indestructible.

The Cathedral was planned in 1812 by Tsar Alexander I to mark the defeat of Napoleon. Consecrated in 1883, Tchaikovsky's famous *1812 Overture* had its debut performance there a year later. Some years after the 1917 revolution, the Soviets blew up the Cathedral. Their intention was to replace it with a monument to socialism to be known as the Palace of Soviets, with a statue of Lenin above it, his hand raised in blessing. The project failed and instead it became a swimming pool. When the godless Soviet system collapsed, the

Russian Orthodox Church was given back the site and the present building was completed in 2000.

Archbishop Anthony Bloom was for many years a leading figure in the Russian Orthodox Church in Britain and Ireland. He spent his early years mainly in Russia and Iran, but following the Russian Revolution the family settled in Paris. He trained as a surgeon and during the Second World War aided the French resistance. Throughout those turbulent times, Bloom remained deeply religious and he was ordained in 1948. Later, reflecting on the effects of the Russian Revolution on the Church, he could see spiritual gain in that wilderness experience: 'During the Revolution we lost the Christ of the great cathedrals, the Christ of the splendidly architected liturgies; and we discovered the Christ who is vulnerable just as we were vulnerable, we discovered the Christ who was rejected as we were rejected, and we discovered the Christ who had nothing at his moment of crisis, not even friends, and this was similar to our experience. God helps us when there is no one else to help. God is there at the breaking point, at the centre of the storm.'

The poet Irina Ratushinskaya lost much more than a building or a liturgy. At the age of twenty-eight she was accused of anti-Soviet propaganda and sentenced to seven years hard labour. Her only crime was writing poetry. In a poem written in the Labour Camp in Barashevo, she describes brutal attempts made to break her: 'From me they have taken my friends and my folk, Torn my cross from its chain and removed my clothes, and then with their boots kicked me senseless, Beating out with prejudice the remnants of hope.' But they could never break this young woman or undermine her deep personal faith. Her determination is reflected in the title of her book of poems, which was smuggled out of prison in 1986 and published in the West: *No, I'm Not Afraid*.

Few of us, if any, will ever endure the sufferings of those who have been tortured and persecuted for their faith. Nevertheless we can be inspired by their courage and their certainty, which are born of the knowledge that God helps us when there is no one else to help in times of personal crisis or loss. That is their experience, and our faith, and our hope.

When we are asked to justify that faith and hope, it is important to note the survival of the Church itself, the worshipping community that lives by God's promises. Alexander Solzhenitsyn tells of a Eucharist he attended while he was a prisoner in the Gulag. In that barren place, a long-imprisoned Orthodox priest conducted the service from memory without vestments or service books as if he were in the grandest of churches. When the priest turned and declared: 'The body of Christ. The blood of Christ.' Solzhenitsyn said he watched the tears of joy on the faces of the prisoners, who held out grimy hands to receive what only the eyes of faith could see, and sip from an unseen chalice what only the soul could taste. For there was no bread or wine to be the body and blood of Jesus that day – and yet the miracle did occur. What Solzhenitsyn experienced in that Eucharist changed his life.

As poor, yet making many rich; as having nothing and yet possessing everything.

(2 Corinthians 6:10)

Jingle Bells

Christmas: a place where faith and culture meet.

Published 14 December 2013

It is easy to lose sight of what the excitement is really about in these busy pre-Christmas weeks.

The street decorations, the chorus of Christmas carols and seasonal songs in the shops, the office parties and perhaps most importantly the family gatherings – all contribute to a festive mood that brightens dark winter days. Some will question the social and commercial emphasis of the festival, believing that not enough attention is paid to its religious importance.

Some years ago, the then Archbishop of Canterbury Robert Runcie addressed that very point:

> I am frankly rather tired of the tendency of Christians to berate the world for its commercialism and lack of appreciation of what the Feast of Christmas is all about.

You know the sort of thing I mean. It's those sermons and parish magazine articles, read curiously by only the most devout, in which Christmas trees are dismissed as pagan cult objects; it's the obsessiveness which bans the singing of any carols before Christmas Eve; it's the encouragement to Christians to challenge the surrounding culture with the 'real message' of Christmas. All this is part and parcel of a tendency within the Christian community to despise the folk festival. My point is not that we should lose the significance and distinctiveness of the Christian calendar but rejoice at the 'rumours of God' which are stirred in the spirit of all people at such times.

But how do we hold on to 'the significance and distinctiveness' of Christmas? That's a real challenge for the Church in a questioning world.

In St Matthew's Gospel (11:2–11) we are told that John the Baptist asked questions of and about Jesus: 'When John heard in prison what the Messiah was doing, he sent word by his disciples and said to him, "Are you the one who is to come, or are we to wait for another?"' It remains a valid question. Who do we believe Jesus to be and what are our expectations of him? It's something that needs to be thought about.

An anonymous writer asks us to consider the following:

He [Jesus] was born in a small village, the son of a peasant woman. He grew up in another village where he worked as a carpenter till the age of thirty. Then, for three years he became a strolling preacher. He never wrote a book, never held a public office. Never had a family or home, never went to university. Never travelled more than 300 kilometres from his place of birth. Never achieved anything that is associated with greatness. Had no credentials other than himself. When he was thirty-three years old public opinion turned against him. His friends abandoned him. He was handed over to his enemies, who made fun of him at a trial. He was crucified between two thieves. Twenty centuries have passed, and today he is the central figure of our world, a decisive factor in the progress of humanity. None of the armies that have marched, none of the navies that have sailed, none of the parliaments that have met, none of the kings that have reigned, not even all of them together have changed the life of men on earth as this solitary life.

People will say that Christmas is only for children or those with families. That may be true if we treat Christmas as an annual social event, with a token Jesus at its centre.

But the real Christmas never ends. Jesus is Emmanuel, God, with us at all times and in all the uncertainties of life: with us, yes, in times of happiness but also in times of need; with us in anxiety, in suffering, in bereavement, in loneliness. Christmas has meaning for everyone, because in a unique way it reveals to us the God who is love. The poet Christina Rossetti wrote:

> Love came down at Christmas,
> Love all lovely, Love Divine,
> Love was born at Christmas,
> Star and Angels gave the sign. …
>
> Love shall be our token,
> Love shall be yours and love be mine,
> Love to God and to all men,
> Love for plea and gift and sign.

The Finger Of Suspicion

In a world where many millions are treated as slaves we are part of the problem and we know it.

Published 5 April 2014

Set in pre-Civil War America, the film *12 Years a Slave* tells the story of a free man living in New York who is abducted and sold into slavery, where he suffers appalling cruelty at the hands of his captors. At this year's Academy Awards festival in Hollywood it won the award for Best Picture. The director of the film, Steve McQueen, ended his acceptance speech with these words: 'I dedicate this award to all the people who have endured slavery. And the 21 million people who still suffer slavery today.'

Last year, in what was Bangladesh's worst ever industrial disaster, over a thousand people lost their lives when a nine-storey building used as a clothes factory collapsed. The victims were poor people, badly paid and working in a building that was unsafe. People across the world were horrified, and the western clothing companies that made huge profits out of these people promised to take more care. But Simon McRay of Ethical Clothing Australia argued that anyone buying cheap clothing must realise that it is cheap for a reason. 'If you're going to buy cheap fashion you're buying exploitation there's no two ways around it.'

In his book *Christians in an Age of Hunger*, Ronald Sider, a Canadian-born theologian, argues that we live in a world of structured injustice:

> Christians frequently restrict the scope of ethics to a narrow class of personal sins. A few years ago in a study of over 1500 clergy it was discovered that the theologically conservative clergy speak out on sins such as drug abuse and sexual misconduct. But they fail to preach about the sins of institutionalised racism, unjust economic structures and militaristic institutions which destroy people just as do alcohol and drugs. There is an important difference between consciously willed individual acts and participation in evil social structures. Slavery is an example of the latter. So is the Victorian factory system where 10-year-old children worked 12 to 16 hours a day. Both slavery and child labour were legal. They destroyed people by the millions. They were institutionalised or structural evils. The Bible condemns both.

We will fail to understand the significance of the events leading up to and including Holy Week if we fail to recognise that the mission of Jesus was directed against 'institutionalised [and] structural evils' which existed at that time. This is what set him on a collision course with the religious and political powers of his day, who saw him as a threat to their interests. Sadly, there is much to suggest that he would be treated in exactly the same way by the world of today.

Passion Sunday, makes an important statement about how Jesus reacted to their hostility. The word 'passion' means more than mere suffering; it means passively accepting suffering and allowing others take control. It is the very opposite of the me-first culture that controls those 'institutionalised or structural evils'. Jesus allows them to do things their way and in doing so he forces them to reveal their true characters.

The Bible teaches that no matter how awful things appear to be, there is no situation under God which cannot be reclaimed. The prophet Ezekiel (Ezekiel 37) is given a vision of the 'dry bones' of Israel, a vision of a nation being given new life by the spirit of God. It demonstrates how a defeated and displaced people, once victims of a brutal empire, can be restored by the power of God.

The Gospel of St John (11:1–45) tells how Lazarus who has died is also given new life. Jesus had been called by Lazarus's sisters when he became ill but Jesus delayed and the man died. The women criticised Jesus for not coming sooner, however, because of that delay we are shown the power of God not only to heal, but also to give new life. It tells us that God can give us more than we ask for if we have the patience to let go and let him.

Believing In An Age Of Science

Science cannot ignore religion no more than religion can ignore science.

Published 22 February 2013

It would be interesting to know what passes through people's minds when they hear those words from the Book of Genesis that introduce the Old Testament account of creation: 'In the beginning God …'

Many today are attracted to the views of scientists like Richard Dawkins, who dismiss any suggestion that there is a God in control of the created order. Dawkins is not the first scientist to think like that. Two hundred years ago, Napoleon asked Laplace, the French astronomer and mathematician, where was God in his scientific system and Laplace replied, 'I do not need God to explain the Universe.' Yet many other scientists, like Dr David Wilkinson, an astrophysicist and theologian, disagree: 'The God Christians believe in is a God who is intimately involved with every moment of the universe's history, not just its beginnings.'

Jonathan Sacks, who was until recently Chief Rabbi of the United Hebrew Congregations of the British Commonwealth, challenges Professor Dawkins and his supporters. Sacks claims that they make a fatal error by not recognising the difference between science and religion: 'Science is about explanation. Religion is about interpretation. Science takes things apart to see how they work. Religion puts things together to see what they mean. They are different intellectual enterprises. They even occupy different hemispheres of the brain.' He considers the mutual hostility between religion and science to be one of the curses of our age and suggests that it is damaging both to religion and science.

The Bible is not overly interested in how the universe began. Dr Sacks points out that the Bible is not proto-science, pseudo-science or myth masquerading as science. It is interested in other questions entirely – Who are we? Why are we here? How shall we live? These are questions that science can never fully answer. To exclude them is to reduce humankind to the status of the robot, devoid of consciousness, feelings or creativity. Women and men have always asked such questions: 'When I consider your heavens, the work of your fingers, the moon and the stars, which you have set in place, what is mankind that you are mindful of them, human beings that you care for them?' (Psalm 8)

Wilkie Au, Professor of Theological Studies at Loyola Marymount University in Los Angeles, suggests that the creation and our part in it is a work in progress:

> Even at the end of a lifetime of effort we still need to be completed by the finishing touch of the divine artist. God will then bring to completion in us the eternal design of people destined to love wholeheartedly. While awaiting that unifying touch of divine grace, we pilgrims are called to follow the way of Jesus. And the Lord who walks with us assures us that we will always

be blessed. A rabbi was once asked 'What is a blessing?' He prefaced his answer with a riddle involving the creation account in Genesis. After finishing his work on each of the first five days, the Bible states 'God saw that it was good.' But God is not reported to have commented on the goodness of what he created on the sixth day when the human person was fashioned. 'What conclusion can you draw from that?' asked the rabbi. Someone volunteered, 'We can conclude that the human person is not good.' 'Possibly' the rabbi nodded 'but that's not a likely explanation.' He then went on to explain that the Hebrew word translated as 'good' in Genesis is the word *tov*, which is better translated as 'complete.' That is why the rabbi contended God did not declare the human person to be *tov*. Human beings are created incomplete. It is our life's vocation to collaborate with our Creator in fulfilling the Christ-potential in each of us.

Scientists and people of faith are like Abraham, the father of faith, who set out 'not knowing where he was going'. But he was sure of one thing – the journey would be worthwhile.

Hard Choices

St Patrick's Day in New York in 2014 was an occasion of controversy.

Published 22 March 2014

It's quite a distance from New York to Sychar, a city that once stood in what we know today as the West Bank: that tragic land, ruled by fear and patrolled by Israeli soldiers was in the time of Jesus called Samaria.

In New York this week there was much talk about being Irish. The Taoiseach took part in the St Patrick's Day parade, a celebration of 'Irishness'; conversely, the Mayor of New York declined to take part because the gay community were not allowed to participate as an identified group.

In the Gospel of St John (4:5–42) we take a journey in time and distance – and perhaps more significantly in understanding – to a well near Sychar. There, Jesus engages with a woman drawing water, thus making an important statement about inclusiveness by crossing every possible social, religious and ethnic boundary. Gender was an issue, as at that time a man could not talk to a woman in the street; race and religion frowned on such contacts. On top of all that, this was a woman with a past and was not seen as very respectable. But Jesus refuses to be bound by traditional barriers – between Jew and Samaritan, between a man and a woman, a rabbi and a sinner. Division by race, creed, class, sex or status is repudiated and instead he asks her for a drink. He will not be restrained by the fears and prejudices of others.

St James's Church near London's Piccadilly Circus takes a similar position:

> We are a Christian community within the Church of England and we take Jesus Christ and the Gospels seriously … We seek to be inclusive, and welcoming of both human experience and human diversity. We take the Bible seriously, and seek to understand it in the light of that same experience and diversity and of what this age knows and Biblical writers did not, and could not, know. Our community is widely representative of partnered and single people, straight and gay, those who have a sure Christian faith and those who struggle with belief.

A recent statement, however, by the English bishops on same-sex marriage and the blessing of gay relationships troubled the rector, the Rev. Lucy Winkett, who responded in a recent sermon:

> The Bishops' pastoral guidance as it is called in fact simply restates everything that has been said before. There is nothing new in what they've said – but the tone and the emphasis on discipline, especially for clergy, is stronger. I know that the tone of the statement has caused hurt, frustration and not a little anger for many in the church … I do feel as Rector here that it is very

important that I reiterate publicly at this juncture that whatever the bishops are saying and however they say it, the strong commitment of this church remains to every person – to you – and every person whether you identify as gay, bisexual, lesbian, trans, and all of you who are not sure or don't know what your label is; as well as every person, every person who is straight, rich or poor, single, partnered, married, curious.

Our commitment is to you when you are in work, out of work, grieving, glad, anxious, contented, despairing, if your mental health is robust, if your mental health is fragile, if you are lonely or in love, or pregnant or wish you were, or worry that you don't want to be, if you're worried about getting older or feeling that you're too young … our commitment simply mirrors God's commitment to you, whoever you are, wherever you come from. It doesn't matter what you are wearing or if you are thin or if you are big, or if you hate yourself or love the sound of your own voice. It does not matter to us because it does not matter to God. Every person, every person, whatever you have done, whoever you want to be, is honoured here and loved and accepted.

It's a very, very long way from New York to Sychar.

Bibliography

Arnold, John, *Life Conquers Death* (Michigan: Zondervan, 2007).

Atwell, Robert (ed.), *Celebrating the Saints: Daily Spiritual Readings for the Calendars of the Church of England, the Church of Ireland, the Scottish Episcopal Church and the Church in Wales* (Norwich: Canterbury Press, 2004).

Austin, Michael, *Exploration in Art, Theology and Imagination* (Sheffield: Equinox Publishing Limited, 2005).

Au, Wilkie, *By Way of the Heart: Toward a Holistic Christian Spirituality* (London: Geoffrey Chapman, 1990).

Barry, F.R., *The Relevance of Christianity* (London: James Nisbett & Co., 1932).

Bassett, Elizabeth, *The Bridge is Love* (London: Darton, Longman and Todd, 1981).

Bloom, Anthony, *Beginning to Pray* (NJ: Paulist Press, 1994).

Bloom, Anthony, *Living Prayer* (London: Darton, Longman and Todd 1966).

Bonhoeffer, Dietrich, *Ethics* (New York: Touchstone, 1955).

Borg, Martin and Crossan, John Dominic, *The Last Week* (London: S.P.C.K., 2008).

Bosanquet, Mary, *The Life and Death of Dietrich Bonhoeffer* (New York: Harper and Row, 1969).

Bryars, Gavin, 'Jesus Blood Never Failed Me Yet', *Gavin Bryars* [website],
http://www.gavinbryars.com/Pages/jesus_blood_never_failed_m.html

Burrows, Ruth, *Ascent to Love*, ed. Elizabeth Ruth Obbard (London: Darton, Longman and Todd, 1980).

Carretto, Carlo, *Letters from the Desert* (London: Darton, Longman and Todd, 1972).

Carter, Jimmy, *Our Endangered Values* (New York: Simon and Schuster, Inc. 2006).

Chung Hyun Kyung, *Struggle to Be the Sun Again: Introducing Asian Women's Theology* (London: SCM Press, 1991).

Church Publishing, *Holy Women, Holy Men* (New York: Church Publishing, 2010).

Dalrymple, John, *Costing Not Less Than Everything* (London: Darton, Longman and Todd, 1975).

Darling, Edward, and Davison, Donald, *Companion to Church Hymnal* (Dublin: Columba Press, 2005).

Doctrine Commission of the Church of England, Stephen Sykes, 2005.

Dorgan, Theo, 'Nobody should be rebuked or mocked for personal beliefs', *The Irish Times*, 18 August 2012.

Elchaninov, Alexander, *The Diary of a Russian Priest* (Faber and Faber, 1967).

Einstein, Alfred, *Mozart: His Character, His Work* (Oxford: Oxford University Press, 1962).

Eliot, T. S., *The Four Quartets* (London: Faber and Faber, 1959).

Fabella, Virginia, 'Symbols in John's Resurrection Scene: Reflections on the Garden and Mary Magdalene' in *Women of Courage: Asian Women Reading the Bible*, ed. Lee Oo Chung et al. (Chennai: Asian Women's Resource Centre for Culture and Theology, 1992).

Fogelman, Eva, *Conscience and Courage: Rescuers of Jews During the Holocaust* (New York: Anchor, 1995).

Fogelman, Eva, 'Rescuers of Jews During the Holocaust: A Model for a Caring Community', *Representations of the Holocaust* [website], http://writing.upenn.edu/~afilreis/holocaust_new/rescuers-article.php

Fromm, Erich, *The Art of Loving* (New York: HarperCollins, Harper Perennial Modern Classics (50th anniversary edition), 2006).

Hastings, Adrian, *Robert Runcie* (London: Mowbray, 1991).

Hastings, Adrian, *The Shaping of Prophecy* (London: Geoffrey Chapman, 1995).

Huddleston, Trevor, *Naught For Your Comfort* (New York: Doubleday & Company, 1956).

Ingrams, Richard, *Jesus: Authors Take Sides* (London: HarperCollins, 1999).

Jenkins, David, *God Miracle and the Church of England* (London: SCM Press, 1987).

Jerome, *128* (a contemporary reading, tr. Jennifer Wild).

Kavanagh, Patrick, *Come Dance with Kitty Stobling and Other Poems* (London: Longmans, 1960).

King Jr, Martin Luther, *Why We Can't Wait* (New York: Harper and Row, 1964).

Lewis, C.S., *Miracles* (London: Geoffrey Bles, 1947).

Lewis, C.S., *Surprised by Joy: The Shape of my Early Life* (Harcourt, Inc., 1955).

Marlowe, Lara, 'Secularists cry heresy as Sarkozy gets religion', *The Irish Times*, 10 March 2008, http://www.irishtimes.com/opinion/secularists-cry-heresy-as-sarkozy-gets-religion-1.901748.

McCarthy, Aidan, *A Doctor's War* (London: Grub Street, 2006).

Martini, Cardinal Carlo Maria, tr. John L. Allen Jr, 'Translated final interview with Martini', *National Catholic Reporter* [website], 4 September 2012, http://ncronline.org/blogs/ncr-today/translated-final-interview-martini

Moriarty, Gerry, 'Spences remembered as "Godly men"', *The Irish Times*, 19 September 2012, http://www.irishtimes.com/news/spences-remembered-as-godly-men-1.737662

Niebuhr, Reinhold, *The Irony of American History* (New York: Scribner Book Co., 1984).

Nouwen, Henri, *The Living Reminder* (London: Harper Collins, 2009).

O'Connor, Elizabeth, *Cry Pain, Cry Hope* (Washington: The Servant Leadership School, 1987).

O'Driscoll, Herbert, *Prayers for the Breaking of Bread* (New York: Cowley Publications, 1991).

O'Driscoll, Herbert, *Praying to the Lord of Life* (Toronto: Anglican Book Centre, 1989).

O'Malley, Austin, *Keystones of Thought* (Harvard: Devin-Asair, 1914).

Priestland, Gerald, *Priestland's Progress: One Man's Search for Christianity Now* (quoting from John Bunyan, *The Pilgrim's Progress*) (BBC Books, 1981).

Pritchard, John, *Living the Gospel Stories Today* (London: SPCK, 2001).

Popham, Peter, *The Lady and the Peacock* (London: Rider, Random House, 2011).

Ratushinskaya, Irina, *Dance with a Shadow*, tr. David McDuff (Newcastle upon Tyne: Bloodaxe Books, 1992).

Romero, Oscar, from a Homily given on Good Friday 1979, *The Church is All of You: Thoughts of Archbishop Oscar Romero*, comp. and tr. James R. Brockman SJ (Winston Press, 1984).

Scott-Holland, Henry, *Facts of Faith* (Longmans & Co.).

Snider, Ronald, *Rich Christians in an Age of Hunger* (Nashville: Thomas Nelson, 2005).

Solzhenitsyn, Alexander, *A Journey Along the Oka* (New York: Farrar, Straus and Giroux, 1971).

Stott, John, *The Message of Acts* (Illinois: InterVarsity Press, 1994).

Stott, John, *Basic Christianity* (Nottingham: IVP Books, 2012).

Taylor, Jeremy, *Holy Living* (1650).

Temple, William, *Readings in St John's Gospel* (Michigan: Macmillan & Co., 1952).

Thomas, R.S., *Poems: 1945–1990* (Australia: Hachette, 2000).

Tolischus, Otto D., "The Pogrom," in *New York Times*, 19 November 1938.

Tutu, Desmond, ed. John Webster, *Crying in the Wilderness* (London: Mowbray, 1990).

Tutu, Naomi, *The Words of Desmond Tutu* (New York: Newmarket Press, 2005).

Van der Post, Laurens, *The Night of the New Moon* (New York: Penguin Putnam, 1977).

Vanier, Jean, *The Broken Body* (London: Darton, Longman and Todd, 1988).

Vulliamy, Ed, 'Bridging the gap, part two', *The Guardian*, 13 July 2008.

Wallis, Jim, *God's Politics* (New York: Harper Collins, 2005).

Wallis, Jim, 'Quran Burning is a Sacrilegious Slap in the Face of Christ', *Sojourners* [website], 9 August 2010, https://sojo.net/articles/quran-burning-sacrilegious-slap-face-christ

Ward, Keith, *Why There Almost Certainly is a God: Doubting Dawkins* (Oxford: Lion Hudson, 2008).

Watson, David, *Fear No Evil: A Personal Struggle with Cancer* (London: Hodder and Stoughton, 1984).

Winkett, Lucy, *Light that Will Not Fade*, Sermon preached 2 March 2014, St James Church, Piccadilly, London.